Practice Bo

ACCESS

Building Literacy Through Learning™

Math

Great Source Education Group

a division of Houghton Mifflin Company

Wilmington, Massachusetts

www.greatsource.com

AUTHORS

Dr. Elva Duran holds a Ph.D. from the University of Oregon in special education and reading disabilities. Duran has been an elementary reading and middle school teacher in Texas and overseas. Currently, she is a professor in the Department of Special Education, Rehabilitation, and School Psychology at California State University, Sacramento, where she teaches beginning reading and language and literacy courses. Duran is co-author of the Leamos Español reading program and has published two textbooks, *Teaching Students with Moderate/Severe Disabilities* and *Systematic Instruction in Reading for Spanish-Speaking Students.*

Jo Gusman grew up in a family of migrants and knows firsthand the complexities surrounding a second-language learner. Gusman's career in bilingual education began in 1974. In 1981, she joined the staff of the Newcomer School in Sacramento. There she developed her brain-based ESL strategies. Her work has garnered national television appearances and awards, including the Presidential Recognition for Excellence in Teaching. Gusman is the author of *Practical Strategies for Accelerating the Literacy Skills and Content Learning of Your ESL Students.* She is a featured video presenter, including "Multiple Intelligences and the Second Language Learner." Currently, she teaches at California State University, Sacramento, and at the Multiple Intelligences Institute at the University of California, Riverside.

Dr. John Shefelbine is a professor in the Department of Teacher Education, California State University, Sacramento. His degrees include a Master of Arts in Teaching in reading and language arts, K-12, from Harvard University and a Ph.D. in educational psychology from Stanford University. During his 11 years as an elementary and middle school teacher, Shefelbine has worked with students from linguistically and culturally diverse populations in Alaska, Arizona, Idaho, and New Mexico. Shefelbine was a contributor to the California Reading Language Arts Framework, the California Reading Initiative, and the California Reading and Literature Project, and has authored a variety of reading materials and programs for developing fluent, confident readers.

EDITORIAL: Developed by Nieman Inc. with Phil LaLeike
DESIGN: Ronan Design

Printed in the United States of America

International Standard Book Number -13: 978-0-669-50899-4
International Standard Book Number -10: 0-669-50899-3
(*Practice Book*)

18 19 20 21 – 0304 – 21 20 19 18
4500729808

International Standard Book Number -13: 978-0-669-51658-6
International Standard Book Number -10: 0-669-51658-9
(*Practice Book, Teacher's Edition*)

4 5 6 7 8 9–1689–14 13 12 11 10

TABLE OF CONTENTS

Whole Numbers

Practice

For Exercises 1–3, tell the place and the value of each 6.

1. 710,063 ______

2. 460,822 ______

3. 186,012,489 ______

For Exercises 4–6, write each number in word form.

4. 394 ______

5. 195,502 ______

6. 825,000,000 ______

For Exercises 7 and 8, write each number in standard form.

7. three hundred nineteen thousand, six hundred eighty-one

______

8. forty-four million, six hundred thousand, ninety-four

______

9. Write a number that is less than 5,809,256 and greater than 5,758,103.

______

For Exercises 10 and 11, use < or > to compare the two numbers.

10. 46,820 and 46,802 ______

11. 33,809,464 and 33,819,460 ______

12. **Multiple Choice** Which number is "thirty million, three hundred twenty-six thousand, nine hundred twelve" in standard form?

A. 30,326 **B.** 3,326,912 **C.** 30,326,912 **D.** 33,026,912

Name ____________________

FOR USE WITH PAGE 20

Develop Language

A. Question and Answer Use pages 16–17 in *ACCESS Math* to complete the chart below.

Standard Form, Word Form, and Whole Numbers

WHAT is a whole number?	WHAT is standard form?	HOW are standard form and word form different?	HOW do I read a whole number in standard form?	HOW do I write a whole number in standard form?

B. Comparing Read the six numbers below. Some are in standard form and others are in word form. Then compare the numbers. Write them all in standard form so they are in order from least to greatest.

five hundred two thousand, nine hundred forty

38,901

112,833

one hundred thirteen thousand, six hundred

39,810

thirty-eight thousand, nine hundred ten

____

____

____

Name ....

Rounding

Practice

For Exercises 1–3, round each number to the underlined place.

1. 32,891 ________ **2.** 55,934 ________ **3.** 35,768,032 ________

4. Plot each number on the number line. Then round each number to the nearest hundred thousand.

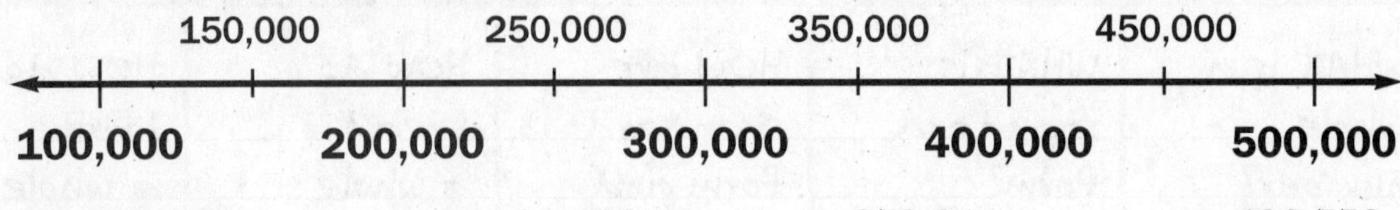

a. 457,290 **b.** 103,199 **c.** 273,911 **d.** 400,772

________ ________ ________ ________

5. Write a number that becomes 375,000 when rounded to the nearest thousand. ________________

6. Trudy wrote a 3-digit whole number. The digits are 3, 6, and 8. When rounded to the nearest hundred, her number becomes 900. What is Trudy's number? ________________

7. Yazmi wrote a 3-digit whole number using digits 1, 4, and 7. When rounded to the nearest hundred, her number becomes 400. What is her number? ________________

8. **Extended Response** Darren's number is 752,819. Round it to the nearest hundred thousand; ten thousand; thousand; hundred; and ten. Then tell how you do it. ________________

____

____

____

Name ____

FOR USE WITH PAGE 25

Develop Language

A. Rounding In the chart below, complete each sentence to explain how to round a 4-digit number to the nearest thousand. Then follow the steps to round each number to the nearest thousand.

Step ① Underline the digit in the ________ place.	Step ② Circle or highlight the digit in the ________ place.	Step ③ Ask, *Is the circled digit* ____ *or greater?*	Step ④ If *yes,* add ___ to the rounding digit. If *no,* don't change the ________ ______.	Step ⑤ Change all digits after the rounding digit to ___.
3,591				
6,242				

B. Interpreting The table shows populations of the five largest cities in Illinois. Round each population to the nearest hundred thousand. Write two or three sentences to interpret the information.

City	Population	Rounded
Rockford	151,068	
Naperville	135,389	
Aurora	156,974	
Chicago	2,886,251	
Joliet	118,423	

Source: *NY Times Almanac 2004*, pp. 178–79.

____

____

____

____

Name

Exponents

Practice

For Exercises 1–4, write each product in exponential form.

1. $3 \times 3 \times 3$ ______

2. $7 \times 7 \times 7 \times 7 \times 7$ ______

3. $10 \times 10 \times 10 \times 10$ ______

4. $45 \times 45 \times 45 \times 45 \times 45 \times 45$ ______

For Exercises 5–8, write each number in expanded form.

5. 6^3 ______ **6.** 2^9 ______

7. 11^2 ______ **8.** 25^4 ______

For Exercises 9–12, find the value of each number.

9. 5^4 ______ **10.** 10^3 ______

11. 12^2 ______ **12.** 2^6 ______

13. In an election for student council, Renee received 5^3 votes, Moira received 3^5 votes, and Edwidge received 4^4 votes. List the three candidates in order of votes received, from greatest to fewest.

______

14. **Short Response** Ivan has 3^4 sports cards in his collection. Nami has 4^3 sports cards in his collection. Cyrus says that he can tell who has more sports cards just by looking at the numbers. How?

______

______

______

______

Name ______________________________

FOR USE WITH PAGE 30

Develop Language

A. Definition Chart Complete the Definition Chart below. Write the definition for each word. Then give an example of each term, or use it in a sentence.

Term	Definition	Example or Sentence
standard form		
expanded form		
exponential form		
factor		
base		
exponent		

B. Predicting Complete the table to show the 2nd, 3rd, 4th, and 5th powers of 2 and 5. Predict whether the 6th power of 2 will be even or odd. Then predict whether the 6th power of 5 will be even or odd. Write your predictions on the lines below. Check your work.

Power of 2	Standard Form	Power of 5	Standard Form
2^1	2	5^1	
2^2		5^2	
2^3		5^3	
2^4		5^4	
2^5		5^5	

____

____

____

Name

Mental Math

Practice

For Exercises 1–4, find each missing number. Then tell which property or properties are shown.

1. $37 + \blacksquare = 52 + 37$ __________

2. $(4 \times 8) + (4 \times 12) = \blacksquare \times (8 + 12)$ __________

3. $15 + (125 + 8) = (15 + \blacksquare) + 8$ __________

4. $(\blacksquare \times 7) \times 35 = 7 \times (2 \times 35)$ __________

For Exercises 5–8, use mental math to find each answer. Then tell which property or strategy you used.

5. 2×39 __________

6. $6 \times 20 \times 5$ __________

7. $38 + 150 + 32$ __________

8. $(7 \times 25) + (3 \times 25)$ __________

For Exercises 9–12, use mental math to find the answer.

9. 34×9 __________ **10.** $585 - 399$ __________

11. $2 \times 61 \times 5$ __________ **12.** $429 + 368$ __________

13. Phoebe had $12.71. She spent $5.99. How much did she have left? Use mental math. __________

14. There are 12 cans of soup in a case. This month, the cafeteria manager ordered 14 cases of soup. Last month, the cafeteria manager ordered 6 cases of soup. How many cans of soup did the manager order in all during the two months? Use mental math to find the answer.

____

15. **Multiple Choice** Which number is equal to $(13 \times 4) + (2 \times 4)$?

A. 60 **B.** 50 **C.** 48 **D.** 25

Name ______________________________

FOR USE WITH PAGE 35

Develop Language

A. Web Complete the Web below. In each oval, write a property or strategy that is useful when solving a problem mentally.

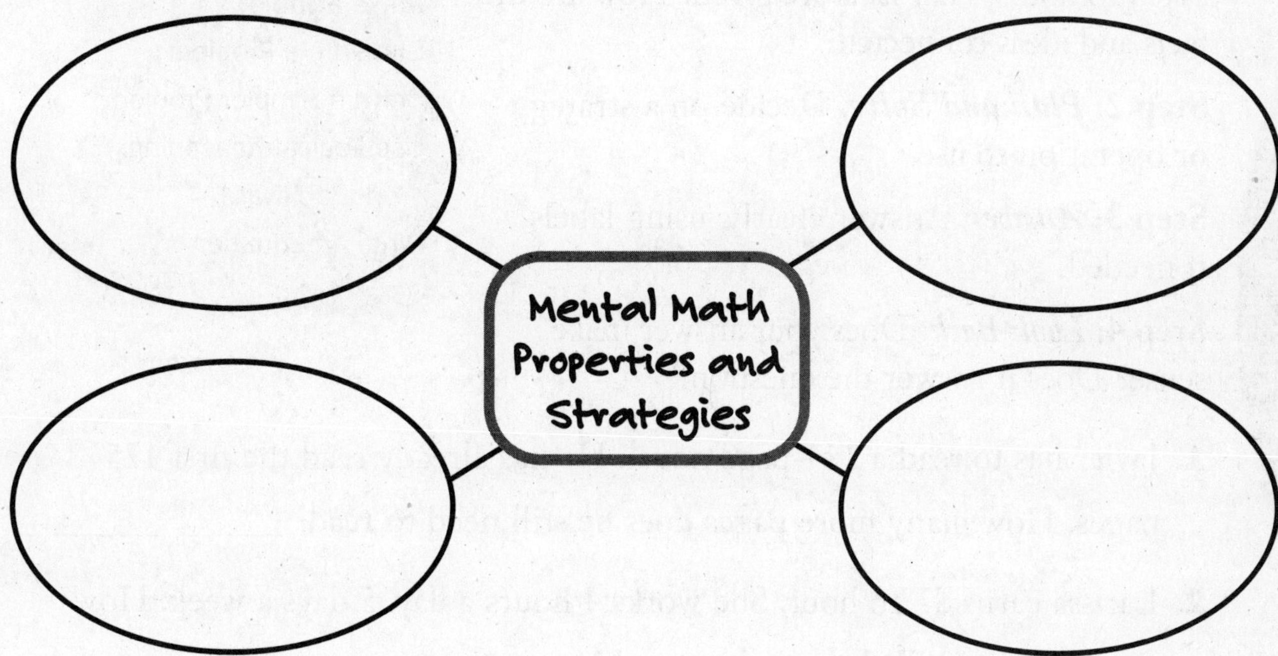

B. Explaining Use mental math to solve each problem. Then explain your thinking. Record the steps you took and the property or strategy you used.

39 + 575 + 25 + 11	(7 × 27) + (27 × 3)	5 × 29
Solution:	Solution:	Solution:
First, I	First, I	First, I
Then, I	Then, I	Then, I

Name

Problem Solving

Use a Problem-Solving Guide

Use this problem-solving guide to solve the problems below. Show your work.

Step 1: *Read and Understand.* What are you asked to find? What facts are given? How are the facts and ideas connected?

Step 2: *Plan and Solve.* Decide on a strategy or operation to use.

Step 3: *Answer*. Answer clearly, using labels if needed.

Step 4: *Look Back.* Does your answer make sense? Does it answer the question?

Problem-Solving Skills

- Draw a Diagram
- Guess, Check, and Revise
- Look for a Pattern
- Make an Organized List
- Make a Model
- Make a Table
- Simulate a Problem
- Solve a Simpler Problem
- Use Logical Reasoning
- Work Backward
- Write an Equation

1. Javier has to read a 244-page novel. He has already read the first 175 pages. How many more pages does he still need to read? ______________

2. Larissa earns $7 an hour. She works 4 hours a day, 5 days a week. How much money will she earn in a week? ______________

3. Will has square tiles that are 3 in. by 3 in. He has a tabletop that measures 1 ft by 1 ft. How many tiles can he put on the tabletop so they fit with no spaces or overlaps? ______________

My Summary of the Unit

Name ____________________

FOR USE WITH PAGES 16–37

Unit Vocabulary

Sentence Frames Each sentence below has two blanks. For each sentence, fill in the first blank with the correct vocabulary term from the Word Bank. Then fill in the second blank with the number that makes the sentence true. When you are finished, add the six numbers you have written. The sum of these numbers should be 100.

Word Bank

- base
- power
- Commutative
- round
- Distributive
- standard form

1. If you ______________ 38 to the nearest ten, it will become ______.

2. Kendra used mental math to find that the value of 2 to the fourth ______________ is ______.

3. According to the ______________ Property, $63 \times 12 =$ ______ $\times 63$.

4. If you write $3 \times 3 \times 3 \times 3$ in exponential form, the ______________ will be 3 and the exponent will be ______.

5. According to the ______________ Property, $(25 \times 3) + (25 \times 7) =$ ______ $\times (3 + 7)$.

6. If you write the number six thousand, two hundred sixty-six in ________________, you will need to use the digit 6 ______ times.

______ + ______ + ______ + ______ + ______ + ______ = 100

Name

Order of Operations

Practice

For Exercises 1–3, simplify each expression. Use the rules for the order of operations.

1. $81 \div (3 + 6) - 5$ ______

2. $(3 \times 5) + (16 \div 2^2)$ ______

3. $5^2 - 4 \times 5$ ______

For Exercises 4–6, write an algebraic expression for each word phrase.

4. 7 less than x ______

5. y divided by 2 ______

6. the number of legs on z cats ______

For Exercises 7 and 8, use parentheses to make each sentence true.

7. $30 \div 5 + 5 \times 4 = 12$ ______

8. $27 + 8 \div 4 + 3 = 5$ ______

9. Use the numbers 2, 3, 4, and 5 once each to make the sentence true.

■ × ■ − ■ ÷ ■ = 13 ______

10. Write a situation that could be described by the expression $5s$.

______

______

11. **Multiple Choice** Simplify $4 + (2^3 - 2) \times 4$.

A. 4 **B.** 28 **C.** 32 **D.** 40

12. **Multiple Choice** Simplify $(4 + 2^3) - 2 \times 4$.

A. 4 **B.** 28 **C.** 32 **D.** 40

Name ______________________________

FOR USE WITH PAGE 42

Develop Language

A. Sequence Complete the chart below. Explain how you would follow the rules for the order of operations to solve the problem on the right. Use these words to help you: *add*, *exponent*, *multiply*, and *parentheses*. Then solve the problem.

$3^2 + (5 - 4) \times 3$

First, I	
Second, I	
Third, I	
Last, I	

B. Choosing an Operation For each situation, choose whether to add, subtract, multiply, or divide to find the answer. Then underline the key words that helped you decide.

1. A guinea pig eats some carrots. Then it eats some more carrots. How many carrots does it eat in all? ______________________

2. Each violin has 4 strings. How many strings are on all the violins in the school orchestra? ______________________

3. Veronica cuts a piece of fabric into 3 equal sections. How long is each piece? ______________________

4. Ranjan spends $5. How much does he have left? ______________________

Name

Expressions

Practice

For Exercises 1–3, evaluate each expression for the given values.

1.

x	$3x$
2	
4	
12	
25	

2.

y	$15 + y$
5	
15	
85	
100	

3.

d	$2d - 8$
5	
7	
10	
30	

For Exercises 4–6, find the rule for each table. Then write an expression for the rule.

4.

m	?
11	15
26	30
40	44
96	100

5.

n	?
3	15
13	65
22	110
50	250

6.

s	?
16	2
24	3
40	5
88	11

______ ______ ______

For Exercises 7–9, find the rule and give the next three terms for each pattern.

7. 7, 14, 21, 28 ______

8. 128, 64, 32, 16 ______

9. 3, 9, 27, 81 ______

10. **Short Response** Mr. Gomez charges $15, plus $2 a mile, for a ride in his cab. Write an expression for the charges, and find out how much it costs for a 12-mile ride. ______

Name ______________________

FOR USE WITH PAGE 47

Develop Language

A. Definition Chart Complete the Definition Chart below. Define each of the terms and give an example.

Term	Definition	Example
variable		
rule		
pattern		
term		
algebraic expression		

B. Evaluating Write *yes* or *no* in the Evaluation Chart below to determine whether each figure on the right is a rectangle.

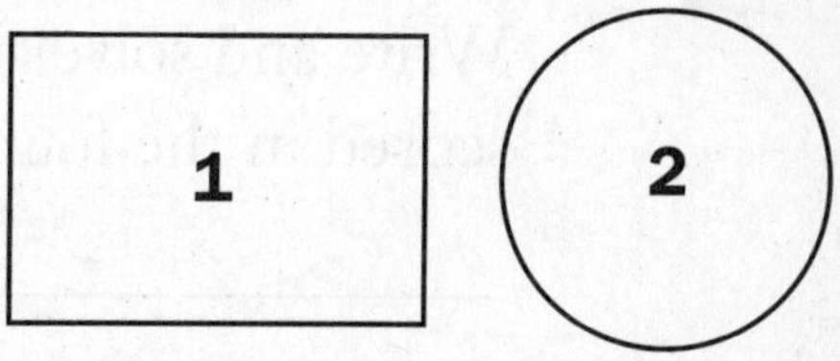

1

2

Criteria for a Rectangle	Evaluation 1	Evaluation 2	Is the figure a rectangle?
Figure has 4 sides.			1 ________
Sides are straight.			
Opposite sides are same length.			2 ________
Angles are all the same size.			

Name

Solving Equations

Practice

For Exercises 1 and 2, tell how to get the variable alone on one side of the equation.

1. $z + 9 = 26$ ____________________

2. $88 = y - 12$ ____________________

For Exercises 3–5, solve each equation. Then check your solution.

3. $30 + n = 42$

4. $m - 5 = 73$

5. $63 = x - 9$

For Exercises 6 and 7, write the equation shown by each diagram. Then solve the equation.

6.

a	14
42	

7.

6	*b*
60	

8. **Short Response** After three quarters of a game, Claudia's basketball team had 57 points. After the fourth quarter, Claudia's team had 72 points. Write and solve an equation to find how many points Claudia's team scored in the fourth quarter.

Name

FOR USE WITH PAGE 52

Develop Language

A. K-W-L Chart Complete the K-W-L Chart below to tell what you know about equations. List what you know about equations, what you want to know about equations, and what you learned about equations. Give examples when you can.

Equations		
What I Know	What I Want to Know	What I Learned

B. Describing Read the equation below. Then describe the steps you can use to solve the equation, and check your answer.

$$18 + y = 34$$

First, I

Second, I

Third, I

Fourth, I

Name

More Equations

Practice

For Exercises 1 and 2, tell how to get the variable alone on one side of the equation.

1. $\frac{a}{4} = 144$ ____________________

2. $117 = 9b$ ____________________

For Exercises 3–5, solve each equation. Then check your solution.

3. $4r = 60$ ____________________

4. $\frac{s}{2} = 96$ ____________________

5. $72 = 6t$ ____________________

For Exercises 6 and 7, write the equation shown by the diagram. Then solve the equation.

6.

m	*m*	*m*	*m*	*m*	*m*
48					

____

7.

n	*n*	*n*
78		

____

8. **Multiple Choice** Wu Kim's computer printer can print 45 pages in 5 minutes. Which equation should you use to find the number of pages Wu Kim's printer can print in 1 minute? Solve the equation.

A. $\frac{p}{45} = 9$ **B.** $\frac{p}{5} = 45$ **C.** $45p = 5$ **D.** $5p = 45$

____

____

Name

FOR USE WITH PAGE 57

Develop Language

A. Question and Answer Use pages 54 and 55 in *ACCESS Math* to complete the chart below.

The Division Property of Equality		
What does it say?	When do you use it?	How is it like the Multiplication Property of Equality?

B. Explaining Use mental math or a Property of Equality to solve each problem below. Explain in writing what you did. Use complete sentences.

$a + 8 = 10$	$7b = 49$	$20 = c - 76$

Name

Problem Solving

Problem-Solving Skills

- Draw a Diagram
- Guess, Check, and Revise
- **Look for a Pattern**
- Make an Organized List
- Make a Model
- Make a Table
- Simulate a Problem
- Solve a Simpler Problem
- Use Logical Reasoning
- Work Backward
- Write an Equation

Look for a Pattern

When you are solving a problem, it can help to look for a pattern in the numbers. Then you can extend the pattern to find the answer. Use the strategy *look for a pattern* to solve these problems.

1. Five people are in a room. Each person shakes hands one time with every other person. How many handshakes are there in all?

____

2. Sabrina uses a pattern to arrange her beads in boxes. She puts 128 beads in the first box, 64 beads in the second box, 32 beads in the third box, and 16 beads in the fourth box. If the pattern continues, which box will have only 1 bead?

____

3. Look at the diagram. If the pattern continues, how many squares will be in the tenth figure?

____

My Summary of the Unit

____

____

____

____

____

____

Name ______________________

FOR USE WITH PAGES 38–59

Unit Vocabulary

Scramble Five vocabulary terms from Unit 2 of *ACCESS Math* are given in the left column below. The names of these terms appear in the right column but their letters are scrambled. Identify the terms and unscramble their names. Write each name on the lines, one letter at a time. Then find the spaces that are starred. Write those letters at the bottom of the page to spell a vocabulary term that means "to find the value of something."

a	brlieava v (*2) _ _ _ _ _ _ (*4) e
$8 + 3^2$ (addition)	tropeaion o _ (*1) _ _ _ _ _ _ _
$5x = 20$	uioatnqe _ q (*5) _ _ _ _ _ n
3, 6, 9, 12, . . .	trentap p (*6) _ _ (*8) _ _ _
( )	ehsenptresa p (*3) _ _ _ _ (*7) _ _ _ _ s

___ (*1) v (*2) ___ (*3) ___ (*4) ___ (*5) ___ (*6) ___ (*7) ___ (*8)

Name

Understanding Decimals

Practice

For Exercises 1–3, use the hundredth grids on the right.

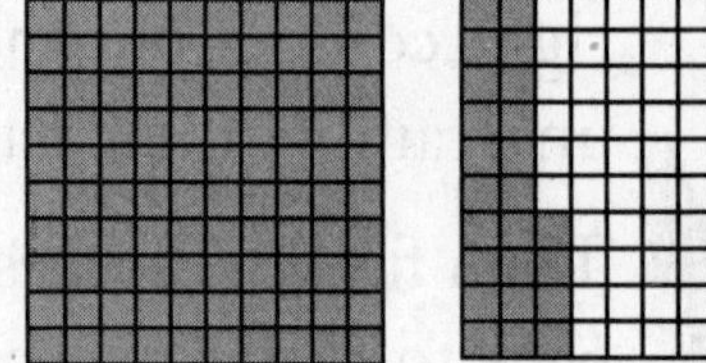

1. What number is shown? Write the answer as a decimal number. ______

2. Write the answer in words.

______

3. Between what two whole numbers is the decimal number?

______

For Exercises 4–6, read aloud the number. Then name the place of the underlined digit, and round the number to that place.

4. 4.<u>8</u>13 ______

5. 7<u>5</u>.9 ______

6. 0.33<u>9</u>2 ______

7. Colin has 3 quarters in one pocket and 7 pennies in another pocket. Write the value of each amount of money as a decimal part of a dollar.

______

8. **Short Response** The diagonal of a 2-inch square is about 2.828427 inches long.

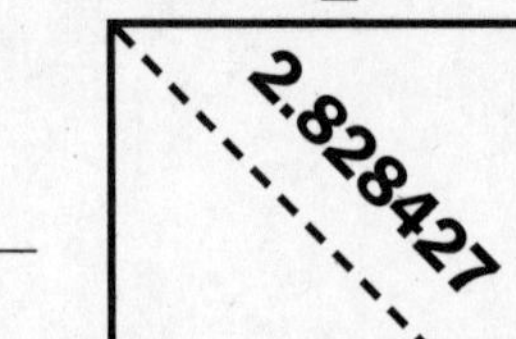

Round 2.828427 to the nearest unit. ______

Round 2.828427 to the nearest tenth. ______

Round 2.828427 to the nearest hundredth. ______

Round 2.828427 to the nearest thousandth. ______

Name ______________________________

FOR USE WITH PAGE 64

Develop Language

A. Web Complete the Web below. In the ovals, write words, phrases, pictures, or examples that are related to decimal numbers.

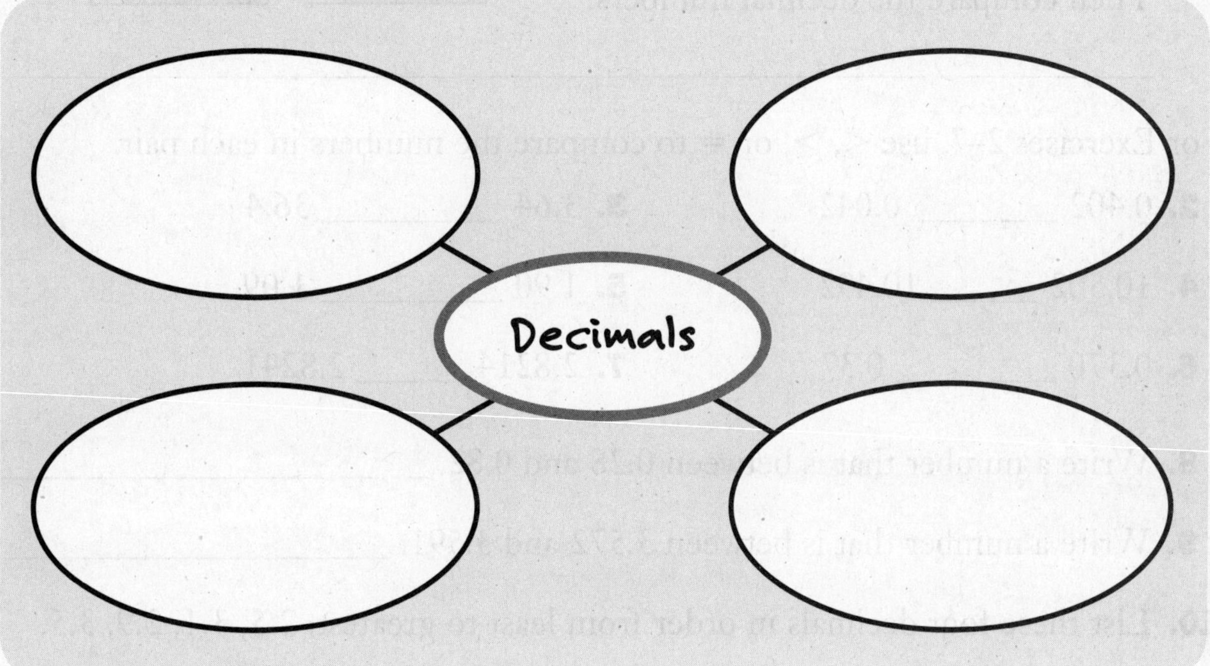

B. Identifying The table below shows the steps for writing a decimal number in word form. The steps are not in the right order. Identify the proper order for the steps. Write the step number in each circle. Then follow the steps to write the decimal numbers below in word form.

Step ◯	Step ◯	Step ◯	Step ◯
Write "and" for the decimal point.	Write the place for the part after the decimal point.	Write the part of the number that is to the right of the decimal point.	Write the part of the number that is to the left of the decimal point.

23.59 ______________________________

150.7 ______________________________

Comparing and Ordering

Practice

Use the models on the right.

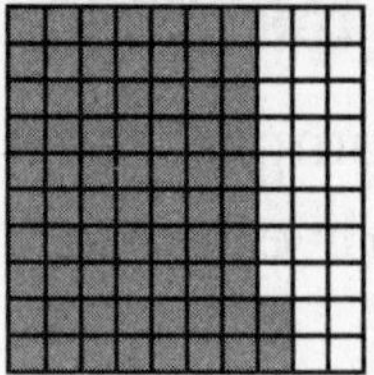
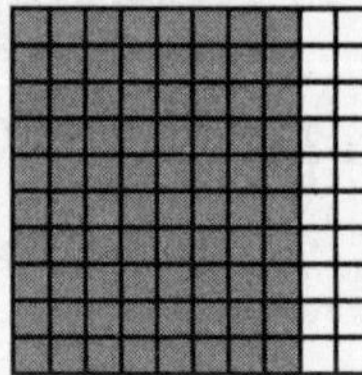

1. Write a decimal number for each model.
Then compare the decimal numbers.

____

For Exercises 2–7, use <, >, or = to compare the numbers in each pair.

2. 0.402 ________ 0.042 **3.** 3.64 ________ 36.4

4. 10.502 ______ 10.492 **5.** 1.90 ________ 1.09

6. 0.370 ________ 0.37 **7.** 2.8214 ______ 2.8241

8. Write a number that is between 0.28 and 0.82. _______________

9. Write a number that is between 3.572 and 3.591. _______________

10. List these four decimals in order from least to greatest: 2.5, 3.1, 2.9, 3.5.

____

11. List these three decimals in order from least to greatest: 0.709, 0.712, 0.710. _______________

12. **Multiple Choice** Which of these decimals is between 0.93 and 0.95?

A. 0.903 **B.** 0.923 **C.** 0.943 **D.** 0.953

Name ______________________________

FOR USE WITH PAGE 69

Develop Language

A. Compare Complete the chart below to tell how to compare two decimal numbers. Circle the word or phrase in parentheses that best completes the sentence. Then follow the steps to compare the two numbers at the bottom of the chart.

First, line up the (last digits/ decimal points).	If needed, put (zeros/ ones) at the end of the number so that the two numbers have the same number of decimal places.	Then, compare the digits, reading from left to right. Stop when you find two digits that are (different / the same).	The number with the greater digit in this place is the (greater/ lesser) number.
42.3052			
42.36			

B. Organizing In 15 minutes, Kaylee roller-skated 2.86 miles, Mercedes skated 2.75 miles, and Ekaterina skated 2.80 miles. The next day, in 15 minutes, Kaylee skated 2.91 miles, Mercedes 2.93 miles, and Ekaterina 3.01 miles.

Organize this information by putting it into the table on the right. Then write two or three sentences describing what you learned about the skaters by comparing the decimals in the data.

	Kaylee	Mercedes	Ekaterina
Day 1			
Day 2			

____

____

____

Name

Adding and Subtracting

Practice

For Exercises 1–6, find each sum or difference.

1. 12.91 + 2.04 ______ **2.** \$0.35 + \$0.79 ______

3. \$16 − \$8.95 ______ **4.** 3.258 + 0.86 ______

5. 13.5 − 2.608 ______ **6.** 18 + 6.717 + 10.49 ______

7. At a rummage sale, Tanisha bought a paperback book for \$1.25, a bracelet for \$2.65, and a bicycle pump for \$3.85. How much change did she receive from a ten-dollar bill? ______

8. Tran bought 5 items at the grocery store. They cost \$1.29, \$4.99, \$2.10, \$0.79, and \$1.18. Round these numbers to the nearest dollar. Then add to estimate the total cost. ______

9. Find two decimal numbers with a sum of 2.45. ______

______

10. Find two decimal numbers with a difference of 2.45.

______

11. The sum of the sides of the triangle on the right is 61.4 m. What is the length of the third side?

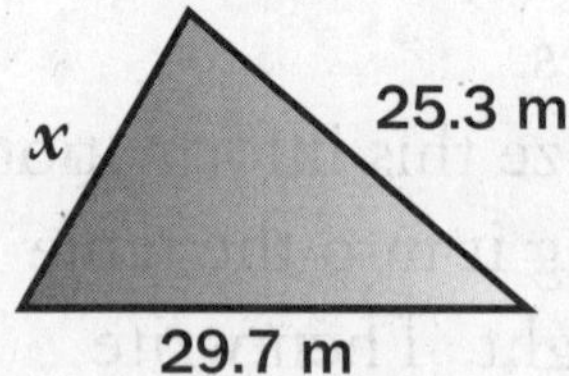

______

12. **Short Response** A student found the sum of 5.25 and 0.4 this way. Tell what the student did wrong. Then solve the problem correctly.

$$\begin{array}{r} 5.25 \\ +\ 0.4 \\ \hline 5.29 \end{array}$$

______

______

Name ______________________________

FOR USE WITH PAGE 74

Develop Language

A. K-W-L Chart Complete the K-W-L Chart below to tell what you know about decimals. List what you know about decimals, what you want to know about decimals, and what you learned about decimals. Give examples when you can.

Decimals		
What I Know	What I Want to Know	What I Learned

B. Summarizing Review the chart above to help you summarize the information that you learned about decimals. Then list terms, skills, and ideas in the table below.

Decimals		
Important Terms	**Important Skills**	**Important Ideas**
1.	1.	1.
2.	2.	2.
3.	3.	3.

Name ____________________

Multiplying and Dividing

Practice

For Exercises 1–4, tell how many digits in the product will be to the right of the decimal point.

1. 5.5×1.7 ____________ **2.** 0.75×3 ____________

3. 0.48×0.22 ____________ **4.** 26.2×153.91 ____________

For Exercises 5 and 6, find each set of quotients.

5. $375 \div 25$ ________ $37.5 \div 25$ ________ $3.75 \div 25$ ________

6. $999 \div 9$ ________ $99.9 \div 0.9$ ________ $9.99 \div 0.09$ ________

For Exercises 7 and 8, rewrite each answer and put the decimal point in the correct position.

7. $4.3 \cdot 1.71 = 7353$ ____________

8. $5.28 \div 0.2 = 264$ ____________

For Exercises 9 and 10, find the quotient or product.

9. $5 \div 0.125$ ____________

10. $0.003 \cdot 1.67$ ____________

11. Enrique earns $6.70 an hour. How much does he earn for working 5.5 hours?

____

12. **Extended Response** How can you use the information that $4.7 \cdot 5 = 23.5$ to help you solve $23.5 \div 0.5$?

____

____

____

____

Name ______________________

FOR USE WITH PAGE 79

Develop Language

A. Definition Chart Complete the Definition Chart below. Define each of the terms and give an example.

Term	Definition	Example
decimal		
product		
quotient		
divisor		

B. Demonstrating Write the steps you would use to multiply 0.36 by 0.2. Then demonstrate how to follow the steps by finding the product.

Steps	Computation
First, I	
Second, I	
Third, I	

Name

Problem Solving

Guess, Check, and Revise

Problem-Solving Skills

- Draw a Diagram
- **Guess, Check, and Revise**
- Look for a Pattern
- Make an Organized List
- Make a Model
- Make a Table
- Simulate a Problem
- Solve a Simpler Problem
- Use Logical Reasoning
- Work Backward
- Write an Equation

Use the strategy *guess, check, and revise* to solve these problems.

1. Tim has a basket filled with oranges and apples. The basket contains 25 pieces of fruit in all. There are 7 more oranges in the basket than there are apples. How many apples are in the basket?

____

2. Mala spent $57 on sandwiches and sodas for her friends. A sandwich cost $5.25 and a soda was $1.50. How many of each did she buy?

____

3. There are 38 animals in a barnyard. Of the 38 animals, some are cows and the rest are chickens. In all, the 38 animals have 124 legs. How many of the animals are cows, and how many are chickens?

____

4. The product of two decimal numbers is 8.12. The difference of the two numbers is 0.1. What are the two numbers?

____

My Summary of the Unit

____

____

____

____

____

____

____

Name ______________________________

FOR USE WITH PAGES 60–81

Unit Vocabulary

Crossword Move the place-value words from the Word Bank into the grid, one letter to a square. Some words will read down and some across. Each word begins in a square with a number. The clues below will help you decide where to put each word.

Across

3. the place of 3 in 56.143

5. the place of 5 in 25.007

6. the place of 6 in 0.631

7. the place of 7 in 7,003.89

Down

1. the place of 1 in 216.7

2. the place of 2 in 0.02

4. the place of 4 in 2,458.9

Word Bank

thousands
hundreds
tens
ones
tenths
hundredths
thousandths

Name ______

Divisibility

Practice

For Exercises 1–4, write the correct word from the Word Bank in each blank. Some words will be used more than once.

Word Bank
factor
multiple
remainder
divisible

1. 24 is not ______ by 5 because
24 ÷ 5 has a ______.

2. 24 is a ______ of 6.

3. 35 has a ______ of 5.

4. 48 is ______ by 12 because 48 ÷ 12 has no ______.

For Exercises 5–8, list three multiples of each number.

5. 4 ______ **6.** 9 ______

7. 10 ______ **8.** 11 ______

For Exercises 9–12, list all factors of each number.

9. 28 ______ **10.** 36 ______

11. 80 ______ **12.** 92 ______

For Exercises 13–16, tell whether each number is divisible by 2, 3, 5, 9, or 10.

13. 84 ______ **14.** 105 ______

15. 90 ______ **16.** 150 ______

17. **Extended Response** If a number is divisible by 10, by which other numbers is it divisible? Explain.

______

______

18. **Short Response** If a number is divisible by 15, by which other numbers is it divisible? ______

Name

FOR USE WITH PAGE 86

Develop Language

A. Divisibility Complete the table below. Tell whether each number in the first column is divisible by 2, 3, 5, 9, or 10. The first number has been done for you. Then explain how you know.

Number	Divisible By	How I Know
45	3, 5, 9	4 + 5 = 9 and 9 is divisible by 3 and 9; 45 ends in 5.
36		
60		
72		
80		

B. Analyzing List the first 10 multiples of 6. Then tell whether each is divisible by 2, 3, 5, 9, or 10. The first three are done for you.

After completing the table, analyze the numbers and complete this sentence:

Every multiple of 6 is also divisible by ______ and ______.

Multiples of 6	6	12	18							
Divisible by	2, 3	2, 3	2, 3, 9							

Name

Prime and Composite

Practice

For Exercises 1–8, tell whether the number is prime or composite.

1. 47 ____________ **2.** 48 ____________

3. 91 ____________ **4.** 87 ____________

5. 53 ____________ **6.** 67 ____________

7. 63 ____________ **8.** 76 ____________

For Exercises 9–16, list the prime factors of the number. Then write the prime factorization using exponents.

9. 16 ____________ **10.** 36 ____________

11. 49 ____________ **12.** 64 ____________

13. 78 ____________ **14.** 80 ____________

15. 108 ____________ **16.** 132 ____________

17. **Extended Response** In the box below, draw two different factor trees for 120. Then write the prime factorization using exponents.

Prime factorization: ____________

18. **Short Response** Why wouldn't you draw a factor tree for the number 23?

____

____

Name ______________________________

FOR USE WITH PAGE 91

Develop Language

A. Sentence Frames Choose a term from the Word Bank to complete each sentence.

Word Bank

- factor trees
- prime numbers
- composite numbers
- prime factorization
- exponents

1. The numbers 5, 13, 19, and 23 are ____________________.

2. ____________________ can help you find the ____________________ of a number.

3. The numbers 12, 56, 82, and 93 are ____________________.

4. In the product $2^3 \cdot 5^4$, 3 and 4 are ____________________.

B. Describing Describe how you would draw a factor tree for 300. Draw your tree in the box on the right.

____

____

____

____

____

____

____

Use your factor tree to help you write the prime factorization of 300 using exponents.

____

____

Name

Greatest Common Factor

Practice

For Exercises 1–8, find all the common factors.

1. 18, 24 ______

2. 32, 40 ______

3. 13, 19 ______

4. 8, 48 ______

5. 30, 50 ______

6. 60, 90 ______

7. 12, 18, 42 ______

8. 32, 64, 72 ______

For Exercises 9–16, find the greatest common factor (GCF).

9. 12, 30 ______

10. 36, 45 ______

11. 24, 60 ______

12. 21, 32 ______

13. 23, 44 ______

14. 15, 90 ______

15. 18, 27, 54 ______

16. 8, 48, 88 ______

Short Response For Exercises 17–20, tell whether the sentence is always true, sometimes true, or never true. Give an example or explanation to support your answer.

17. Two even numbers have a common factor of 3.

______

18. Two odd numbers have a common factor of 3.

______

19. Two prime numbers greater than 2 have 2 as a common factor.

______

20. The GCF of two prime numbers is 1.

______

Name ______________________

FOR USE WITH PAGE 96

Develop Language

A. Factors Two ways to find the greatest common factor of 36 and 48 are shown below. Write two or three sentences to explain each method. Use terms such as *common factors*, *prime factors*, *prime factorization*, and *greatest common factor.*

Factors of 36: (1), (2), (3), (4), (6), 9, (12), 18, 36

Factors of 48: (1), (2), (3), (4), (6), 8, (12), 16, 24, 48

GCF: 12

____

____

____

36 = (2) • (2) • (3) • 3

48 = (2) • (2) • 2 • 2 • (3)

GCF: 2 • 2 • 3 = 12

____

____

____

B. Responding Joe's friend Susie says that the GCF of two numbers is always the lesser of the two numbers. Joe knows that this is not true. Write two or three sentences, with examples, to show how Joe could respond to Susie's statement.

____

____

____

____

____

Name

Least Common Multiple

Practice

For Exercises 1–8, find the first three common multiples.

1. 5, 6 ____________ **2.** 6, 12 ____________

3. 3, 5 ____________ **4.** 8, 10 ____________

5. 9, 12 ____________ **6.** 3, 8 ____________

7. 6, 10, 15 ____________ **8.** 3, 4, 8 ____________

For Exercises 9–16, find the least common multiple (LCM).

9. 12, 30 ____________ **10.** 9, 12 ____________

11. 18, 24 ____________ **12.** 7, 9 ____________

13. 5, 11 ____________ **14.** 15, 90 ____________

15. 12, 18, 27 ____________ **16.** 8, 12, 24 ____________

For Exercises 17 and 18, tell whether the sentence is always true, sometimes true, or never true.

17. The LCM of two prime numbers is the product of the two numbers.

____

18. The LCM of two numbers with no common factors is the greater of the two numbers. ____________

Short Response For Exercises 19 and 20, think of two numbers such that one number is a multiple of the other.

19. What is their greatest common factor? ____________

20. What is their least common multiple? ____________

Name ______________________

FOR USE WITH PAGE 101

Develop Language

A. Multiples Shown below are two ways to find the least common multiple of 10 and 12. Write two or three sentences to explain each method. Use phrases such as *common multiple* and *least common multiple.*

Multiples of 10: 10, 20, 30, 40, 50, (60), 70, 80, 90, 100, 110, (120), 130, . . .
Multiples of 12: 12, 24, 36, 48, (60), 72, 84, 96, 108, (120), 132, . . .
LCM: 60

____

____

____

10 = 2 • (5)
12 = (2 • 2) • (3)
LCM: 2 • 2 • 3 • 5 = 60

____

____

____

B. Persuading Your committee wants the same number of daisies and carnations for table decorations. Daisies come in bunches of 18, and carnations come in bunches of 24. What is the least number of each flower you can buy and have the same number of both kinds? Write two or three sentences to persuade the other committee members that you are right.

____

____

____

____

Name

FOR USE WITH PAGES 102–103

Problem Solving

Make an Organized List

Many times, the best way to solve a problem is to *make an organized list* of all the possibilities and then to identify those that are solutions.

Problem-Solving Skills

- Draw a Diagram
- Guess, Check, and Revise
- Look for a Pattern
- **Make an Organized List**
- Make a Model
- Make a Table
- Simulate a Problem
- Solve a Simpler Problem
- Use Logical Reasoning
- Work Backward
- Write an Equation

1. Nancy needs to set the three numbers on her bicycle lock. She wants to use the numbers 2, 5, and 6. List all the possible combinations she can use. Numbers may be used more than once.

____

____

____

____

2. Hermione needs to make a 65¢ phone call at a pay phone that does not take pennies or half dollars. List the combinations of coins that she can use. Use Q for quarters, D for dimes, and N for nickels.

____

____

3. Cindy's four daughters have names beginning with A, C, E, and T. How many ways can the four letters be arranged on Cindy's license plate?

____

My Summary of the Unit

____

____

____

____

____

____

____

____

Name

FOR USE WITH PAGES 82–103

Unit Vocabulary

Make the Match Match the definitions on the left to the terms on the right. Then write the letters in order on the blanks at the bottom of the page to form two new words.

Definition	Blank	Term
a. product of a whole number and a number greater than zero	____	factor
e. greatest number that is a factor of two or more numbers	____	multiple
f. whole number with more than two factors	____	remainder
g. diagram that shows the prime factors of a number	____	divisible
h. can be divided without a remainder	____	composite number
i. whole number greater than 1; only factors are 1 and itself	____	prime number
m. number that divides another number without a remainder	____	factor tree
r. number that tells how many equal factors are in a product	____	prime factorization
s. least number that is a multiple of two or more numbers	____	exponent
t. amount left after dividing	____	greatest common factor
u. product of prime numbers	____	least common multiple

____ ____ ____ ____ ____ ____ ____ ____ ____ ____ ____

Name

Understanding Fractions

Practice

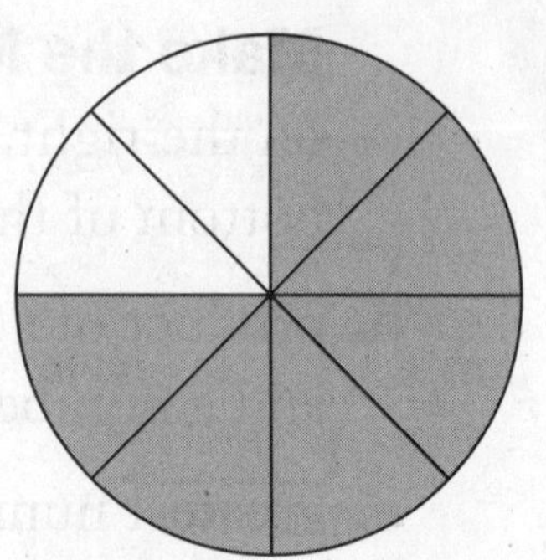

For Exercises 1 and 2, use the diagram on the right.

1. Name the fraction for the shaded portion. ________

2. Write this fraction in simplest form. ________

For Exercises 3–5, use the number line below.

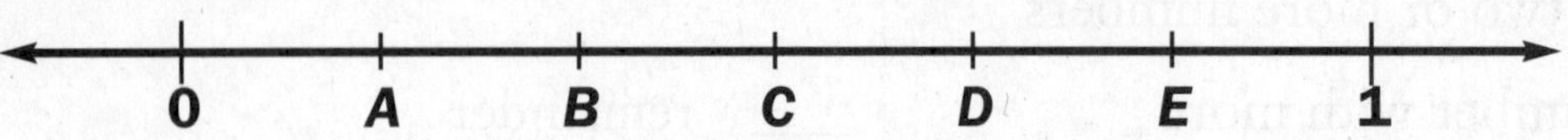

3. What fraction is represented by point *A*? ________

4. What fraction is represented by point *E*? ________

5. Which point shows a fraction equivalent to $\frac{2}{3}$? ____

6. Find the missing number: $\frac{1}{5} = \frac{4}{?}$ ________.

7. Find the missing number: $\frac{6}{27} = \frac{?}{9}$ ________.

8. Tanya has 10 carrots. She eats 3 carrots. What fraction of the carrots is left? ________

9. Find the fraction of the letters in the name STUART that are vowels. Write it in simplest form. ________

10. **Short Response** Gary tosses a coin 20 times. The coin lands heads up $\frac{11}{20}$ of the time. What fraction of the time does the coin land tails up? Tell how you know. ________

____

____

Name ______________________________

FOR USE WITH PAGE 108

Develop Language

A. Alike and Different Complete the chart below to tell how the two terms are alike and different.

Term #1	Term #2	How are they alike?	How are they different?
fraction	decimal		
numerator	denominator		
equivalent fractions	simplest form		
common factor	greatest common factor		

B. Explaining Andi, Bob, Chan, and Diego each ran for 5 minutes. The table shows how far each person ran. Interpret the table by telling which people ran the same distance. You can do this by finding which fractions are equivalent. Then explain how you found the answer.

Person	Distance
Andi	$\frac{6}{10}$ mile
Bob	$\frac{4}{8}$ mile
Chan	$\frac{3}{5}$ mile
Diego	$\frac{12}{20}$ mile

____

____

____

Name ______________________________ FOR USE WITH PAGES 109–112

Mixed Numbers

Practice

For Exercises 1–6, write each improper fraction as a mixed or whole number. Write all fractions in simplest form.

1. $\frac{15}{4}$ ______________ **2.** $\frac{7}{3}$ ______________

3. $\frac{28}{7}$ ______________ **4.** $\frac{14}{12}$ ______________

5. $\frac{13}{2}$ ______________ **6.** $\frac{22}{8}$ ______________

For Exercises 7–12, write each mixed number as an improper fraction.

7. $1\frac{7}{8}$ ______________ **8.** $8\frac{1}{10}$ ______________

9. $3\frac{3}{5}$ ______________ **10.** $2\frac{5}{7}$ ______________

11. $1\frac{6}{9}$ ______________ **12.** $10\frac{1}{2}$ ______________

13. Write a mixed number greater than $3\frac{1}{4}$. ______________

14. Write a mixed number less than $\frac{11}{5}$. ______________

15. Write 17 as an improper fraction. ______________

16. Which is heavier, 3 bricks that weigh $1\frac{3}{4}$ kg each or 4 bricks that weigh $1\frac{1}{4}$ kg each? ______________

17. Darren put 5 erasers side by side. Each eraser is $\frac{3}{8}$ inch long. How many inches long is the row? Write your answer as a mixed number. ______________

18. **Multiple Choice** Suri needs to measure $2\frac{1}{2}$ cups of flour for a recipe. How many times will she need to fill a $\frac{1}{4}$-cup measure?

A. 3 **B.** 5 **C.** 10 **D.** 20

Name ____________________

FOR USE WITH PAGE 113

Develop Language

A. Web Use the Web below to describe mixed numbers. In the ovals, write words, examples, or other information about mixed numbers.

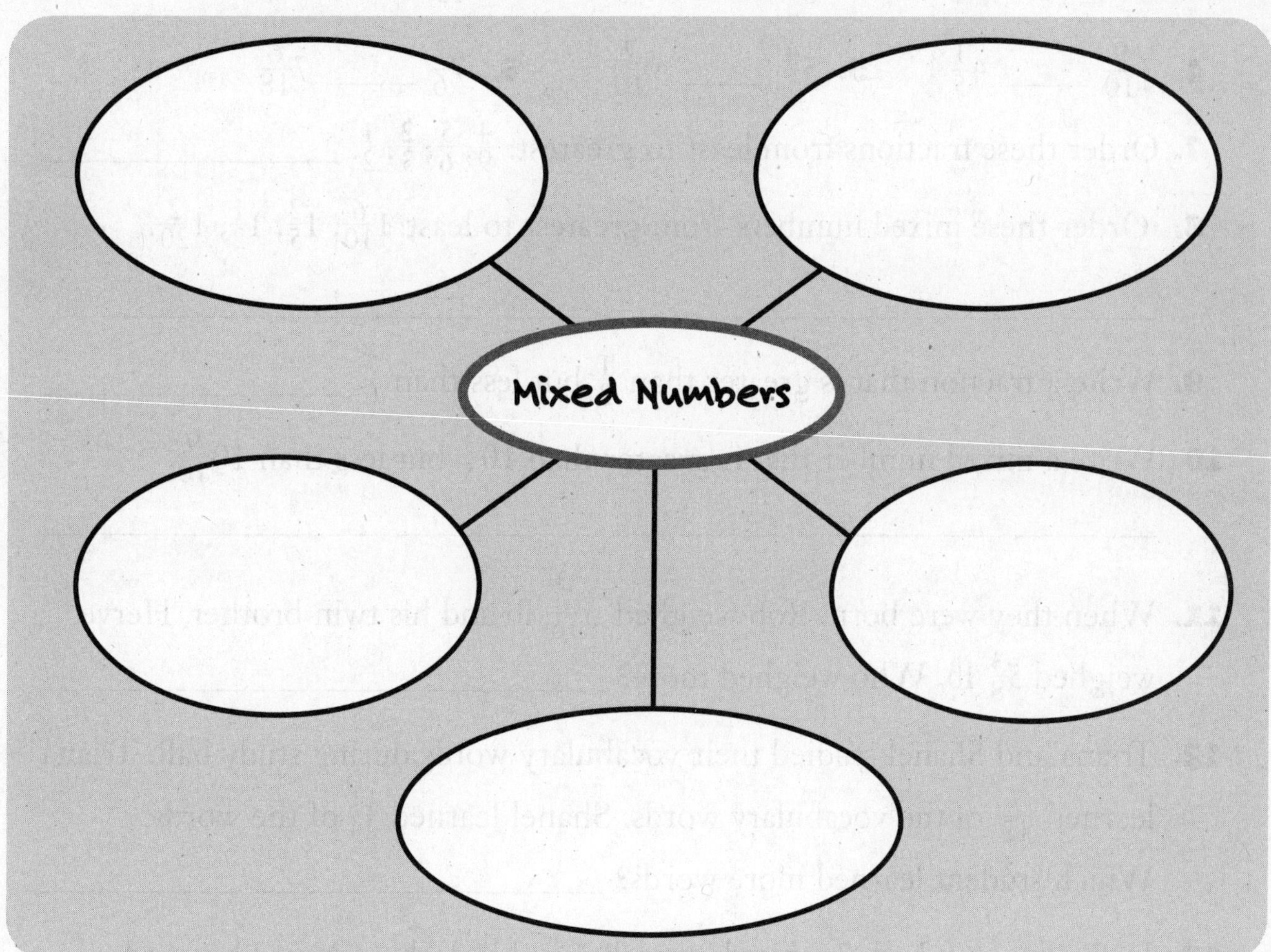

B. Describing Choose two of your examples from the circles above. For each example, write a sentence to describe what it shows about mixed numbers.

1. ____________________

____

2. ____________________

____

Name

Comparing and Ordering

Practice

For Exercises 1–8, write <, >, or =.

1. $\frac{5}{8}$ ______ $\frac{3}{4}$ **2.** $\frac{4}{6}$ ______ $\frac{2}{5}$ **3.** $\frac{3}{12}$ ______ $\frac{2}{8}$

4. $3\frac{9}{10}$ ______ $4\frac{1}{5}$ **5.** $5\frac{4}{5}$ ______ $5\frac{2}{10}$ **6.** $7\frac{2}{6}$ ______ $7\frac{6}{18}$

7. Order these fractions from least to greatest: $\frac{4}{9}, \frac{5}{6}, \frac{2}{3}, \frac{1}{2}$. ______

8. Order these mixed numbers from greatest to least: $1\frac{6}{10}, 1\frac{2}{5}, 1\frac{1}{2}, 1\frac{2}{20}$.

______

9. Write a fraction that is greater than $\frac{1}{2}$ but less than $\frac{7}{8}$. ______

10. Write a mixed number that is greater than $10\frac{3}{5}$ but less than $10\frac{9}{10}$.

______

11. When they were born, Rob weighed $5\frac{7}{16}$ lb and his twin brother, Herve, weighed $5\frac{3}{8}$ lb. Who weighed more? ______

12. Triana and Shanel studied their vocabulary words during study hall. Triana learned $\frac{7}{12}$ of the vocabulary words. Shanel learned $\frac{11}{24}$ of the words. Which student learned more words? ______

13. In the banquet hall, 7 tables have yellow tablecloths, 6 have blue, and 8 have green. What fraction of the tablecloths is blue? ______

14. **Short Response** Write a mixed number that is greater than $6\frac{3}{7}$ but less than $6\frac{9}{14}$. Use simplest form. Then tell how you chose the number.

______

______

______

Name

FOR USE WITH PAGE 118

Develop Language

A. Definition Chart Complete the Definition Chart below. Define each term and give an example.

Term	Definition	Example Sentence
greatest		
least		
compare		
equal		

B. Comparing In the boxes below, show two different ways of comparing the fractions $\frac{3}{8}$, $\frac{1}{4}$, and $\frac{5}{6}$.

Name ....

Adding Fractions

Practice

For Exercises 1–8, find the sum. Give the answer in simplest form.

1. $\frac{3}{16} + \frac{7}{16}$ ____________

2. $\frac{7}{10} + \frac{1}{5}$ ____________

3. $3\frac{1}{3} + 5\frac{4}{5}$ ____________

4. $1\frac{4}{9} + 3\frac{1}{2}$ ____________

5. $\frac{5}{6} + 2\frac{2}{12}$ ____________

6. $1\frac{7}{9} + 3\frac{8}{9} + 2\frac{5}{9}$ ____________

7. $\frac{3}{8} + \frac{1}{16} + \frac{3}{4}$ ____________

8. $2\frac{4}{7} + \frac{3}{7} + \frac{1}{14}$ ____________

9. Write the addition sentence shown by the model. Then find the sum. Give the answer in simplest form.

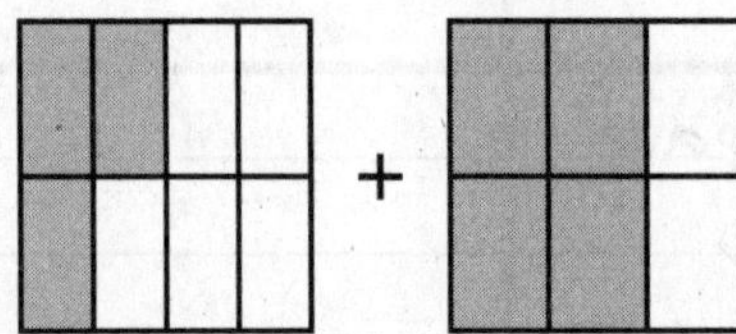

____

10. Jamila ran two laps around the track. She ran the first lap in $24\frac{3}{10}$ sec and the second lap in $25\frac{3}{5}$ sec. How long did she run in all? ____________

11. Of Taylor's postcards, $\frac{2}{7}$ are from Mexico and $\frac{5}{14}$ are from Nicaragua. What fraction of his postcards comes from Mexico and Nicaragua? ____________

12. **Short Response** Which is greater, $\frac{1}{3} + \frac{3}{4}$ or $\frac{5}{6} + \frac{1}{4}$? Explain how you know.

____

____

____

____

____

____

____

Name

FOR USE WITH PAGE 123

Develop Language

A. Sequence Complete the table below. The first row has been done for you.

① Read aloud the expression.	② Find a common denominator.	③ Rename one or both fractions.	④ Add the fractions.	⑤ Rename the sum, if necessary.
$\frac{2}{5} + \frac{1}{10}$	tenths	$\frac{4}{10} + \frac{1}{10}$	$\frac{5}{10}$	$\frac{1}{2}$
$\frac{1}{2} + \frac{3}{8}$				
$\frac{2}{3} + \frac{3}{4}$				

B. Comparing and Contrasting Find $1\frac{4}{5} + 1\frac{2}{5}$. Then find $\frac{3}{4} + \frac{1}{5}$. Use words and drawings to compare and contrast how you found each sum.

Compare	Contrast

Name ____________________

Subtracting Fractions

Practice

For Exercises 1–8, find the difference. Give the answer in simplest form.

1. $\frac{4}{5} - \frac{2}{5}$ ____________ **2.** $\frac{6}{9} - \frac{1}{3}$ ____________

3. $\frac{5}{7} - \frac{1}{2}$ ____________ **4.** $5\frac{9}{10} - 2\frac{1}{10}$ ____________

5. $8\frac{7}{8} - \frac{3}{4}$ ____________ **6.** $1\frac{5}{6} - 1\frac{8}{12}$ ____________

7. $2\frac{1}{5} - 1\frac{1}{3}$ ____________ **8.** $9\frac{1}{5} - 5\frac{1}{4}$ ____________

9. Write the subtraction sentence shown by the model. Then find the difference. Give the answer in simplest form.

____

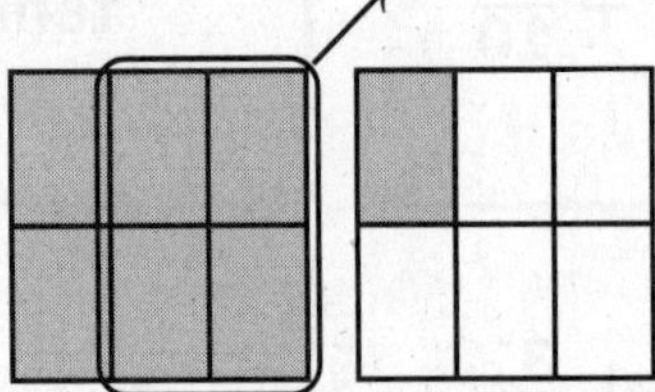

10. Hamid's bookmark is $4\frac{7}{8}$ inches long. Jela's bookmark is $5\frac{1}{4}$ inches long. How much longer is Jela's bookmark than Hamid's? ____________

11. What number completes this sentence: $1\frac{2}{5} - \blacksquare = \frac{1}{10}$? ____________

12. **Extended Response** Find the difference: $4\frac{5}{9} - 2\frac{2}{3}$. Then find two other fractions or mixed numbers with the same difference. Tell how you did it.

____

____

____

____

____

____

____

Name ______________________________ FOR USE WITH PAGE 128

Develop Language

A. Venn Diagram Compare subtracting fractions to subtracting whole numbers by completing the Venn Diagram below. Give examples.

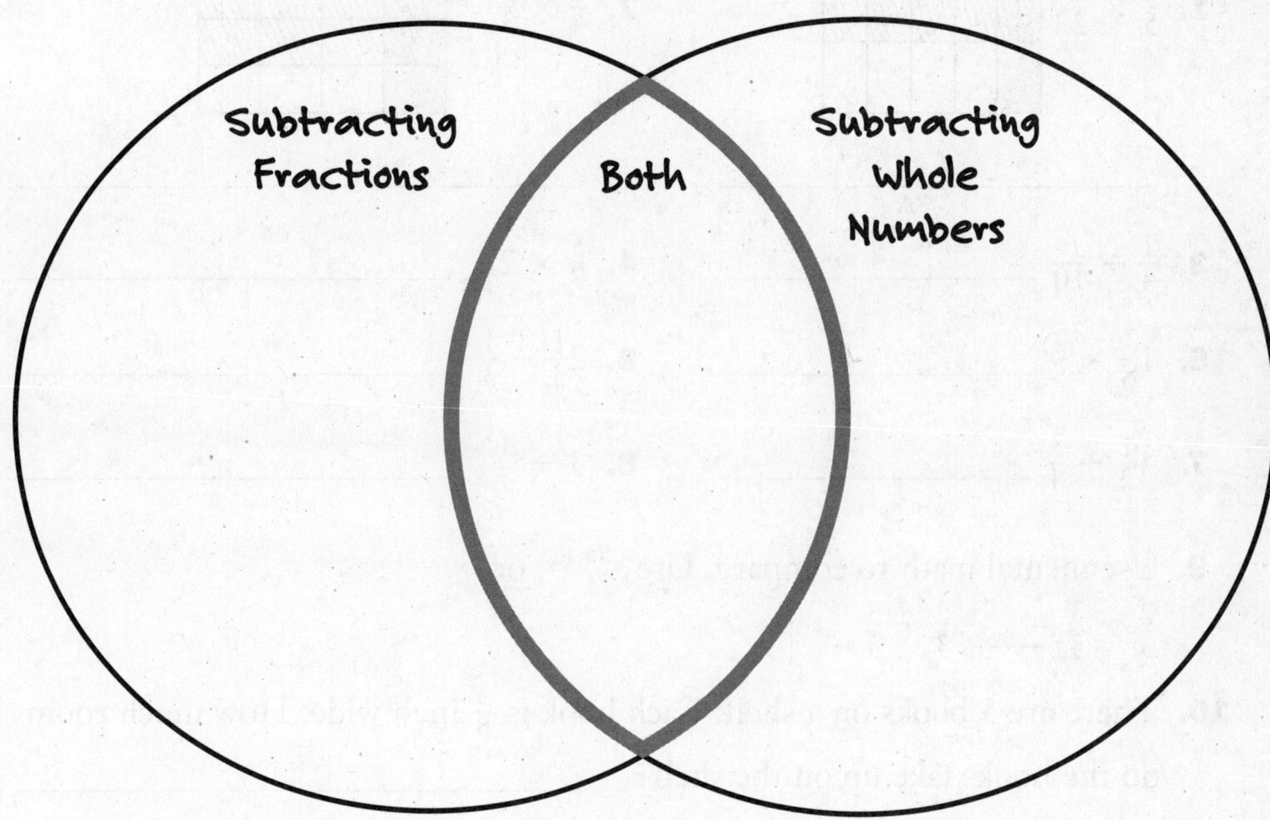

B. Demonstrating Use the rectangles below to demonstrate how to subtract $1\frac{3}{8} - \frac{1}{4}$. Then explain what you did.

Name

Multiplying and Dividing

Practice

For Exercises 1–8, find the product or quotient. Write the answer in simplest form.

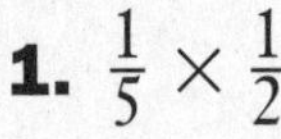

1. $\frac{1}{5} \times \frac{1}{2}$  ______

2. $\frac{1}{4} \times \frac{2}{3}$ 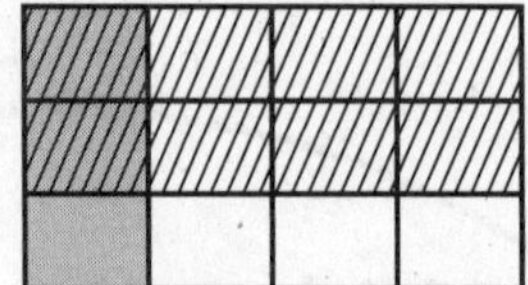 ______

3. $\frac{1}{4} \div \frac{6}{10}$ ______

4. $\frac{5}{7} \times 2$ ______

5. $1\frac{3}{8} \times \frac{2}{5}$ ______

6. $2\frac{1}{3} \div \frac{1}{3}$ ______

7. $4\frac{1}{2} \div \frac{3}{4}$ ______

8. $3 \div \frac{3}{5}$ ______

9. Use mental math to compare. Use <, =, or >.
$\frac{2}{3} \times \frac{3}{5}$ ______ $\frac{2}{3} \div \frac{3}{5}$

10. There are 5 books on a shelf. Each book is $\frac{3}{8}$ inch wide. How much room do the books take up on the shelf? ______

11. Hans drew a line 6 inches long. He divided the line into sections that are each $1\frac{1}{2}$ inches long. How many sections did he have? ______

12. **Extended Response** Simplify $\frac{2}{3} \times \frac{1}{6}$ and $\frac{2}{6} \times \frac{1}{3}$. Then compare the products. What do you notice?

______

______

______

______

______

Name

FOR USE WITH PAGE 133

Develop Language

A. Definition Chart Complete the Definition Chart below. Define each term and give an example.

Term	Definition	Example
fraction model		
quotient		
reciprocal		
mixed number		

B. Clarifying Clarify how to divide $\frac{4}{5}$ by $\frac{3}{10}$ by telling what to do in each step.

1. $\frac{4}{5} \div \frac{3}{10} = \frac{4}{5} \times \frac{10}{3}$

2. $\frac{4}{5} \times \frac{10}{3} = \frac{4 \times 10}{5 \times 3}$

3. $\frac{4 \times 10}{5 \times 3} = \frac{40}{15}$

4. $\frac{40}{15} = \frac{8}{3}$, or $2\frac{2}{3}$

Name

Problem Solving

Work Backward

Sometimes math questions give the ending of a problem but not the beginning. Then you can solve the problem by using the strategy *work backward.*

Problem-Solving Skills

- Draw a Diagram
- Guess, Check, and Revise
- Look for a Pattern
- Make an Organized List
- Make a Model
- Make a Table
- Simulate a Problem
- Solve a Simpler Problem
- Use Logical Reasoning
- **Work Backward**
- Write an Equation

1. Geraldo had a length of ribbon. First, he cut off $1\frac{3}{8}$ inches of the ribbon for an art project. Then, he cut off $3\frac{3}{4}$ inches for his sister. The part of the ribbon that was left over was $5\frac{1}{2}$ inches long. How long was the ribbon to start? ______________________

2. Hanh, Viraj, and C. J. are having bicycle races. Viraj wins $\frac{1}{4}$ of the races. C. J. wins $\frac{3}{8}$ of the races. What fraction of the races does Hanh win? __________ If the boys race 16 times in all, how many races should Hanh expect to win? ______________________

3. When Adam shook the coconut tree, half of the coconuts fell to the ground. When Lee shook the tree, half of the remaining coconuts fell. When Maria shook the tree, 3 coconuts fell. There were 12 coconuts left on the tree. How many coconuts were on the tree to start? Explain.

____

____

My Summary of the Unit

Name ______________________________ FOR USE WITH PAGES 104–135

Unit Vocabulary

Mystery Word Each definition below matches a vocabulary term from the Word Bank. Write the vocabulary words, one letter to a space, on the lines provided. Then read the boxes from top to bottom. You will spell out another important math term.

Word Bank

- denominator
- fraction
- mixed number
- numerator
- quotient
- reciprocal
- simplest form

1. The bottom number in a fraction, which tells how many equal parts there are in all

2. A number written as the sum of a whole number and a fraction

3. The number by which another number is multiplied to get the product 1

4. The answer to a division problem

5. The top number in a fraction, which tells how many equal parts are being considered

6. A number that describes part of something

7. Lowest terms

1. [ ] _ _ _ _ _ _ _ _ _ _

2. _ _ _ _ [ ] _ _ _ _ _

3. _ _ [ ] _ _ _ _ _ _ _

4. _ _ _ _ [ ] _ _ _

5. _ _ [ ] _ _ _ _ _ _

6. _ _ [ ] _ _ _ _ _

7. _ _ _ _ _ [ ] _ _ _ _ _ _ _

Ratios and Proportions

Practice

For Exercises 1–4, find a ratio equal to the one given.

1. $\frac{8}{6}$ ____________ **2.** $\frac{36}{12}$ ____________

3. $\frac{7}{35}$ ____________ **4.** $\frac{9}{10}$ ____________

For Exercises 5–10, solve each proportion.

5. $\frac{12}{20} = \frac{n}{10}$ ____________ **6.** $\frac{5}{6} = \frac{25}{x}$ ____________

7. $\frac{80}{m} = \frac{4}{5}$ ____________ **8.** $\frac{33}{99} = \frac{a}{6}$ ____________

9. $\frac{n}{8} = \frac{96}{128}$ ____________ **10.** $\frac{360}{x} = \frac{100}{5}$ ____________

11. Do the ratios $\frac{7}{3}$ and $\frac{9}{12}$ form a proportion? Explain why or why not.

____

12. Do the ratios $\frac{10}{15}$ and $\frac{4}{6}$ form a proportion? Explain why or why not.

____

13. Gaston plays baseball. He gets two hits in every 7 times at bat. How many hits would you expect him to get in 77 times at bat? ____________

For Exercises 14 and 15, circle the two ratios that form a proportion.

14. $\frac{4}{9}, \frac{2}{5}, \frac{12}{15}, \frac{12}{27}$ **15.** $\frac{3}{5}, \frac{6}{7}, \frac{24}{28}, \frac{24}{35}$

16. **Short Response** Mr. Foster drives 18 miles in 20 minutes. Ms. Garcia drives 14 miles in 15 minutes. Who drives at a faster rate of speed? Tell how you know.

____

____

____

____

Name ______________________

FOR USE WITH PAGE 140

Develop Language

A. Definition Chart Complete the Definition Chart below. Define each term and give an example.

Term	Definition	Example
ratio		
proportion		
rate		

B. Evaluating The table shows how many goals some soccer teams scored and allowed. Evaluate the information in the table to decide which team has the best ratio of goals scored to goals allowed. Explain how you made your choice.

Team	Goals Scored / Goals Allowed
Lions	$\frac{9}{6}$
Bears	$\frac{12}{8}$
Tigers	$\frac{10}{4}$
Hawks	$\frac{6}{3}$

Name

Understanding Percent

Practice

For Exercises 1–3, tell what percent of each figure is shaded. Then write each percent as a fraction in simplest form and as a decimal.

1. 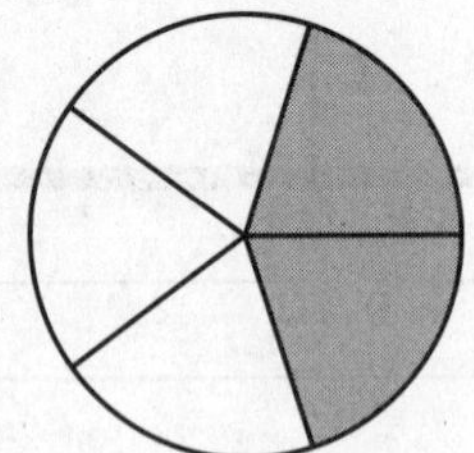

2. 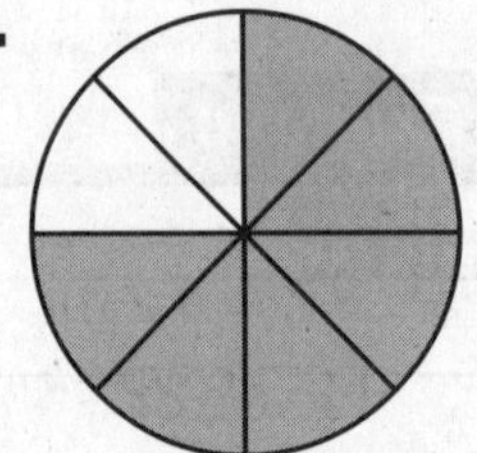

3. 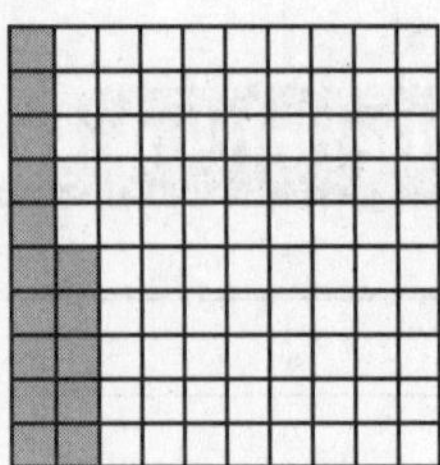

For Exercises 4–7, write each decimal as a percent and as a fraction in simplest form.

4. 0.25 ______

5. 0.9 ______

6. 0.68 ______

7. 0.36 ______

8. Is $\frac{6}{10}$ repeating or terminating? ______ $\frac{6}{11}$? ______

9. Which is greater: $\frac{2}{5}$ or $\frac{4}{9}$? Write both fractions to percents to help you decide. ______

10. **Extended Response** Write 0.7 and 0.07 as percents. Then complete the hundredths grids.

______ ______

Name ____________________

FOR USE WITH PAGE 145

Develop Language

A. Steps Complete the chart below.

How to Change . . .	Step ①	Step ②
25% to a fraction		
38% to a decimal		
0.83 to a fraction		
0.74 to a percent		

B. Predicting Joao sees 80 cars on Tuesday. Of these cars, $\frac{2}{5}$ are red. How many red cars does he see? ________ What percent of the cars that he sees are red? ________ If Joao sees 50 cars on Wednesday, about how many red cars would he expect to see? Explain your prediction.

Name

Percent of a Number

Practice

For Exercises 1–6, write each percent as a decimal and as a fraction in lowest terms.

1. 0.75% ____________ **2.** 3.5% ____________

3. 150% ____________ **4.** 400% ____________

5. 0.5% ____________ **6.** 87.5% ____________

7. Write $\frac{5}{1,000}$ as a percent. ____________

8. Write 3.89 as a percent ____________

For Exercises 9–14, find the percent.

9. 25% of 28 ____________ **10.** $33\frac{1}{3}$% of 153 ____________

11. 150% of 220 ____________ **12.** 0.05% of 5,000 ____________

13. 3.5% of 70 ____________ **14.** 20% of 18.5 ____________

15. Of the 40 students in Mr. Damien's class, 35% speak Spanish. How many students in Mr. Damien's class speak Spanish? ____________

16. **Multiple Choice** Which of these amounts is greatest? Tell how you solved the problem.

A. 25% of 32 **B.** 250% of 4 **C.** 2.5% of 360

____

____

____

____

Name ____________________

FOR USE WITH PAGE 150

Develop Language

A. Order and Draw Write these percents in the correct boxes below to sort them by size. Then complete the hundredths grids to show one of the percents from each box.

0.03%; 250%; 12%; 120%; 2.5%; 0.9%; 0.5%; 25%; 32%; 140%; 0.01%; 90%; 9%; 500%; 0.25%

Less than 1%	From 1% to 100%	Greater than 100%

B. Persuading Ms. Caruso likes suspense movies. Of the 2,000 movies at Jo's Video Shop, 17% are suspense movies. Of the 1,500 movies at Video World, 22% are suspense movies. Where should Ms. Caruso go to find a movie if she wants the largest number of suspense movies to choose from? Write two or three sentences to persuade Ms. Caruso that your idea is right.

____

____

____

____

Name

Applications of Percent

Practice

For Exercises 1–3, find the sale price with the discount.

1. \$16; 25% ____________ **2.** \$69; $33\frac{1}{3}$% ____________

3. \$150; 20% ____________ **4.** \$48; 10% ____________

For Exercises 5–8, find the total cost with the tax.

5. \$40; 5% ____________ **6.** \$92; 4.5% ____________

7. \$2,500; 6.25% ____________ **8.** \$160; 7.5% ____________

9. Mr. and Mrs. Kim go out for lunch. Their bill is \$26. What is their total cost if they add on a 15% tip? ____________ A 20% tip? ____________

10. Leah bought a sweater priced at \$44. The sales tax is 5%. What is Leah's total cost? ____________ The sales clerk's commission is 2.5% of the \$44. How much is the commission? ____________

11. Julio's parents put \$2,000 in the bank at 3% simple interest. How much interest will they earn in 6 years? ____________ Suppose they earn 4.5% simple interest. How much interest will they earn in 3 years? ____________

12. **Short Response** Kate buys a car for \$2,200 with a 5% discount. She figures the total cost by finding 95% of \$2,200, instead of subtracting 5% of \$2,200 from \$2,200. Does her method work? Explain.

____

____

____

____

____

Name

FOR USE WITH PAGE 155

Develop Language

A. Definition Chart Complete the Definition Chart below. Define each term and give an example.

Term	Definition	Example Sentence
tip		
tax		
simple interest		
commission		
discount		

B. Summarizing Use the diagrams below to summarize how each pair of vocabulary terms is alike and different.

Taxes and Discounts	

Tips and Commissions	

Name

Problem Solving

Use Logical Reasoning

Use *logical reasoning* to solve these problems.

Problem-Solving Skills
- Draw a Diagram
- Guess, Check, and Revise
- Look for a Pattern
- Make an Organized List
- Make a Model
- Make a Table
- Simulate a Problem
- Solve a Simpler Problem
- **Use Logical Reasoning**
- Work Backward
- Write an Equation

1. Jane, Hamish, Ivan, and Clara are standing in order of height, with the shortest person in front. Hamish is shorter than Clara, but he is not the shortest of the four. Ivan is standing directly behind Jane. In what order are they standing?

____

2. There are 26 students in Ms. McGirr's class. Of these students, 12 are wearing sneakers and 8 are wearing sweaters. Ten students are wearing neither sneakers nor sweaters. How many students are wearing both sneakers and sweaters?

____

3. Myriam is thinking of a number. Her number is less than 37 and greater than 27. It is not a prime number. It is not evenly divisible by 3. It is odd. What is Myriam's number?

____

My Summary of the Unit

____

____

____

____

____

____

____

____

____

____

____

Name ____________________

FOR USE WITH PAGES 136–157

Unit Vocabulary

Word Search Read the definitions below. Then find each word in the grid that matches the definition and write it on the line with the same number. You can start on any letter and then move up, down, right, or left to the next letter. Connect the letters in each word with a loop. You may use each letter in as many words as you like. You will use every letter. Some letters appear in more than one word.

1. A percent of a bill paid to someone who provides a service
2. A pair of numbers compared by division
3. A ratio with different units of measure
4. One of the two parts of a ratio
5. A statement that two ratios are equal
6. The number of hundredths representing the part of a whole
7. Money paid on a savings account or on borrowed money
8. A percent of the cost of an item, paid to governments
9. An amount taken off the cost of an item

R	O	P	O	R	X
P	N	O	I	T	A
M	R	E	P	E	R
S	T	T	N	E	C
E	R	E	I	D	I
T	N	U	O	C	S

1. ____________________
2. ____________________
3. ____________________
4. ____________________
5. ____________________
6. ____________________
7. ____________________
8. ____________________
9. ____________________

Name

Organizing Data

Practice

Trees in Tariq's Yard

Elm	Pine	Oak
		X
X		X
X		X
X	X	X
X	X	X
X	X	X

Use the line plot for Exercises 1–4.

1. What information is given in the line plot?

2. How many elm trees are in Tariq's yard?

3. How many trees in all are recorded in the line plot?

4. What is the range of the data set?

5. Read this sentence: "THERE ARE THREE TREES HERE." Make a frequency table to show how often each letter appears in the sentence.

Letters	Tally	Frequency
T		
H		
E		
R		
A		
S		

6. **Short Response** Kristin and Cody went bowling. Kristin's scores were 124, 122, 123, 125, and 124. Cody's scores were 91, 123, 108, 108, and 136. Compare and contrast their scores.

Compare	Contrast

Name ______________________________ FOR USE WITH PAGE 162

Develop Language

A. Venn Diagram Complete the Venn Diagram below to compare and contrast frequency tables and line plots. Think about how they are alike and how they are different. Then write your ideas in the diagram.

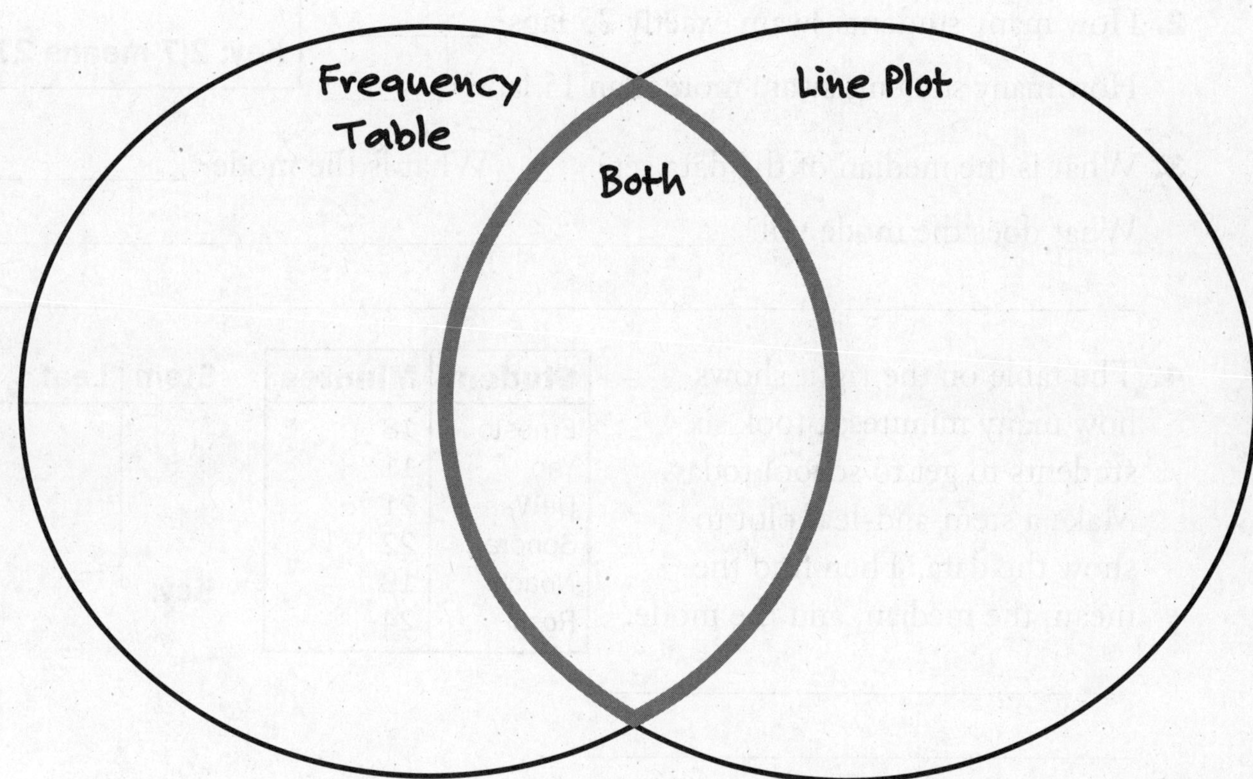

B. Gathering Data Gather data by doing an experiment. First, toss two coins 24 times. Use the frequency table to record the result of each toss. Let H stand for heads and T stand for tails. Then, make a line plot to show your data. Finally, write one or two sentences to summarize the data.

Tossing 2 Coins

Result	Tally	Frequency
HH		
HT		
TH		
TT		

Name ______

Analyzing Data

Practice

Use the stem-and-leaf plot on the right for Exercises 1–4.

Laps Swum Thursday

Stem	Leaf
1	1 3 3 3 6
2	2 5 5 7
3	1 4

Key: 2|7 means 27

1. What was the least number of laps swum by any student on Thursday? _____ The greatest? _____

2. How many students swam exactly 25 laps? _____
How many students swam more than 15 laps? _____

3. What is the median of the data set? _____ What is the mode? _____
What does the mode tell? _____

4. The table on the right shows how many minutes it took six students to get to school today. Make a stem-and-leaf plot to show the data. Then find the mean, the median, and the mode.

Student	Minutes
Ernesto	18
Yao	11
DeWan	21
Sondra	22
Noach	18
Ross	24

Stem	Leaf

Key:

_____

_____

For Exercises 5 and 6, use this information: Ming bought 5 CDs. They cost $14, $17, $14, $15, and $35.

5. Which data item is an outlier? How do you know? _____

6. **Short Response** Find the mean, the median, and the mode of these data.
Which number best represents the data? Why? _____

Name

FOR USE WITH PAGE 167

Develop Language

A. Web Complete the Web below to tell what you know about stem-and-leaf plots. Write your ideas in the circles.

B. Analyzing Analyze these two data sets that show five students' scores on spelling and science tests. Use mean, median, mode, and range to help you. Then write two or three sentences that tell how the data sets are alike and different.

Scores on the Spelling Test
74
99
75
85
75

Scores on the Science Test
91
89
83
96
91

Name

Bar and Line Graphs

Practice

For Exercises 1–3, use the bar graph on the right.

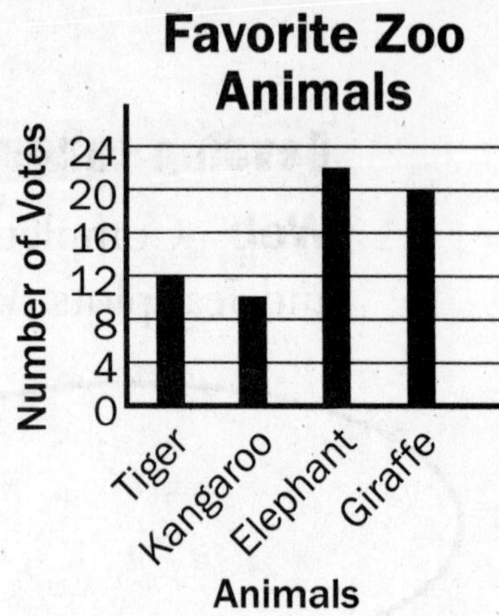

1. What interval was used for this graph?

2. Which animal received the most votes?

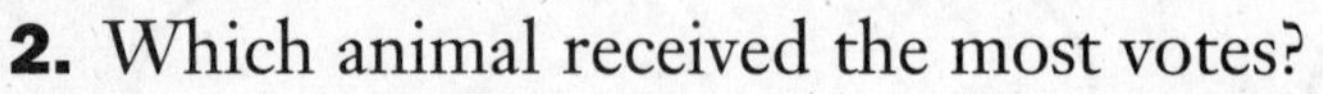

Which was second?

3. How many more students voted for giraffes than voted for tigers?

For Exercises 4–7, use the line graph.

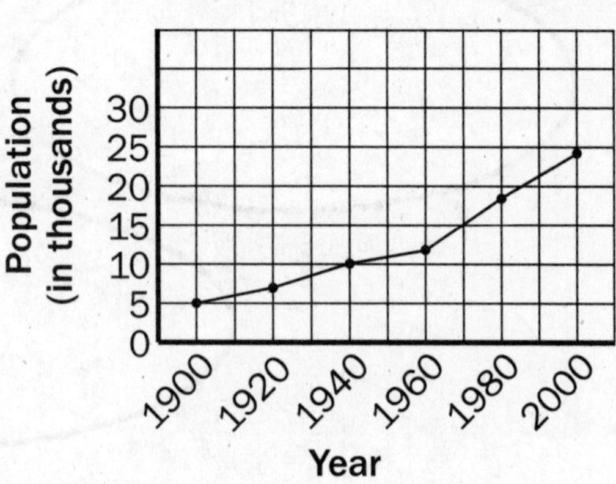

4. What is the title of the graph?

5. About how many people lived in Midland in 1960?

6. What is the trend of the graph?

7. Choose five states. In the box on the right, make a bar graph that shows the number of letters in their names. Use an interval other than 1.

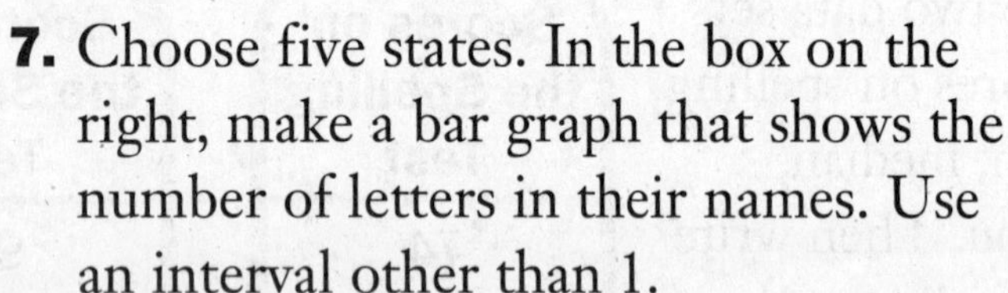

8. **Extended Response** In Exercise 7, why use a bar graph instead of a line graph? Describe a good data set for a line graph.

Name ______________________

FOR USE WITH PAGE 172

Develop Language

A. Definition Chart Complete the Definition Chart below. Define each term and give an example.

Term	Definition	Example Sentence
line graph		
bar graph		
scale		
interval		
trend		

B. Interpreting Interpret the rainfall graph. Think about which months had the greatest rainfall and which had the least. Identify the trends in the graph. Then write two or three sentences describing the data.

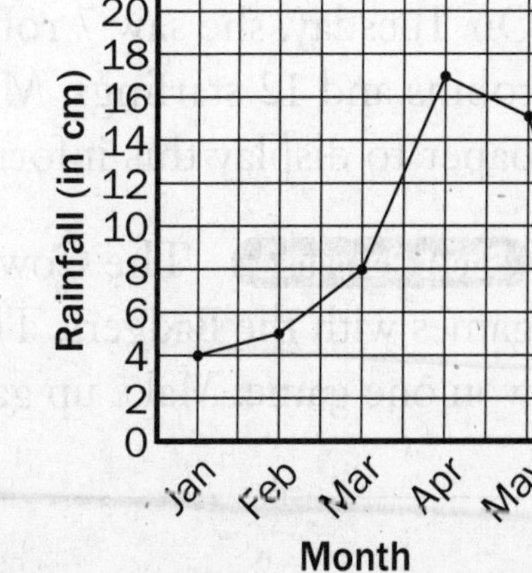

Name

Double Bar Graphs

Practice

For Exercises 1–5, use the double bar graph on the right.

Favorite Sport

Key: ■ girls □ boys

Number of Students: 0, 5, 10, 15, 20

Swimming, Soccer, Bicycling, Baseball

Sport

1. What does the vertical axis show?

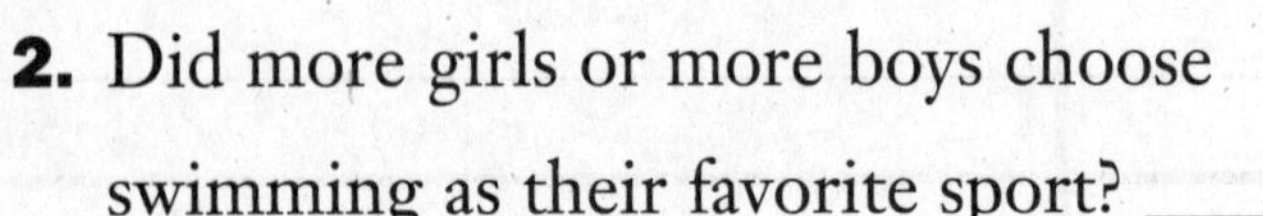

2. Did more girls or more boys choose swimming as their favorite sport? ________

3. Which sport was chosen by the greatest number of boys? ____________

By the greatest number of girls? ____________

4. Which sport was chosen by the same number of boys as girls? ____________

5. How many girls are represented in the graph?

6. Tell how the graph on the right is misleading.

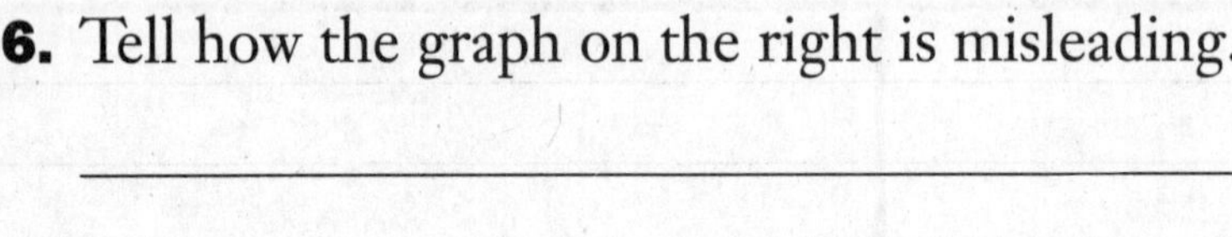

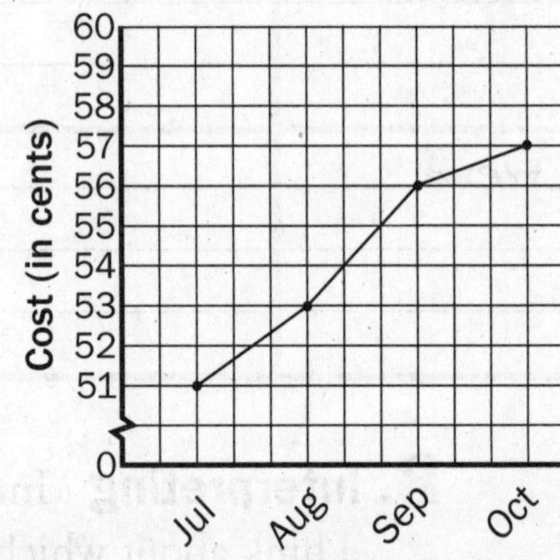

7. On Monday, Derrida saw 15 robins and 5 starlings. On Tuesday, she saw 7 robins and 5 starlings. On Wednesday, she saw 10 robins and 12 starlings. Make a double bar graph on a separate piece of paper to display this information.

8. **Short Response** The Cowboys scored a mean of 60 points in two basketball games with the Badgers. The Badgers scored a mean of 40 points. Each team won one game. Make up game scores that show how this happened.

Name ______________________

FOR USE WITH PAGE 177

Develop Language

A. Question and Answer Complete the chart below. Refer to Lesson 30 in *ACCESS Math* if you need help.

Double Bar Graphs

WHAT is a double bar graph?	WHEN do I use a double bar graph?	HOW do I make a double bar graph?

B. Contrasting The double bar graph on the right shows the average monthly temperatures in Twinsburg and Fallsburg. Study the graph. Then write two or three sentences contrasting the weather in the two towns. Remember, *contrast* means to tell how two things are different.

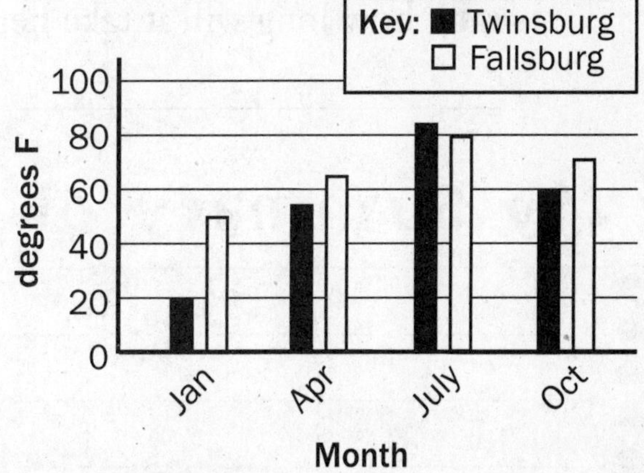

Name

Problem Solving

Make a Table

Use the strategy *make a table* to help you organize information and solve problems. After you have made the table, look for a pattern. Then use the table to extend the pattern.

Problem-Solving Skills

- Draw a Diagram
- Guess, Check, and Revise
- Look for a Pattern
- Make an Organized List
- Make a Model
- **Make a Table**
- Simulate a Problem
- Solve a Simpler Problem
- Use Logical Reasoning
- Work Backward
- Write an Equation

1. Ms. Herrero wants to buy some dinner plates. She can buy a set of 8 plates for $52.98. Then each additional plate costs $8.25. How much will it cost to buy 12 plates?

2. Deanna goes running. It takes her 8 minutes to run the first 1,000 meters and 7 minutes to run the next 1,000 meters. After that, she runs at a rate of 6 minutes for every 1,000 meters. How long will it take her to run 10,000 meters?

3. Mandy is climbing a banana tree to pick bananas. She climbs 3 feet in 15 seconds. Then she rests for 5 seconds and slides down 1 foot. At that rate, how long will it take her to climb 11 feet?

My Summary of the Unit

Name ____

FOR USE WITH PAGES 158–179

Unit Vocabulary

Word Scramble Each picture shows a different way of organizing data. The names of the organizers are scrambled, and each name has one extra letter.

First unscramble the names and write the letters on the lines. Then circle the extra letters and arrange them to spell an important vocabulary term.

Favorite Take-out Food

FOOD	TALLY	FREQUENCY
Hamburger	//	2
Pizza	////	4
Taco	///	3
Fried rice	////	4
Quesadilla	~~////~~ /	6

aqeyfrnceu bleta

__ __ __ __ __ __ __ __ __

__ __ __ __ __

Favorite Sport
Key: shaded = girls, empty = boys
Number of Students: 0, 5, 10, 15, 20
Swimming, Soccer, Bicycling, Baseball
Sport

ulbode rba pragnh __ __ __ __ __ __

__ __ __   __ __ __ __ __

Trees in Tariq's Yard

Elm	Pine	Oak
X X X X X	X X X	X X X X X X X

niel telop

__ __ __ __   __ __ __ __

Laps Swum Thursday

Stem	Leaf
1	1, 3, 3, 3, 6
2	2, 5, 5, 7
3	1, 4

Key: 2|7 means 27

tmes-dan-fela lptod

__ __ __ __ - __ __ __ -

__ __ __ __   __ __ __ __ __

Favorite Zoo Animals
Number of Votes: 0, 4, 8, 12, 16, 20, 24
Tiger, Kangaroo, Elephant, Giraffe
Animals

ambr hrapg

__ __ __   __ __ __ __ __

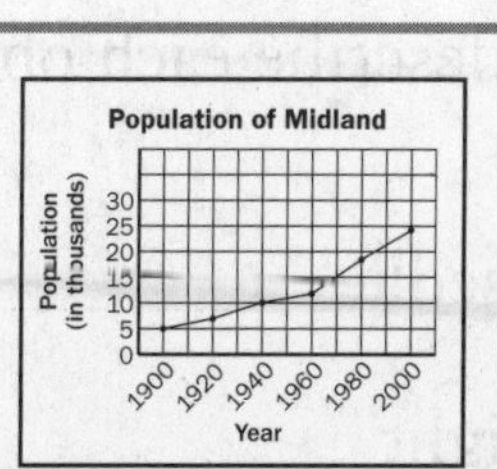

ieiln arghp __ __ __ __   __ __ __ __ __

Extra letters: __ __ __ __ __ __ __

Vocabulary word: ______________

Name ______________________

Lines and Angles

Practice

For Exercises 1–4, use the diagram on the right. Write the angles that match the descriptions.

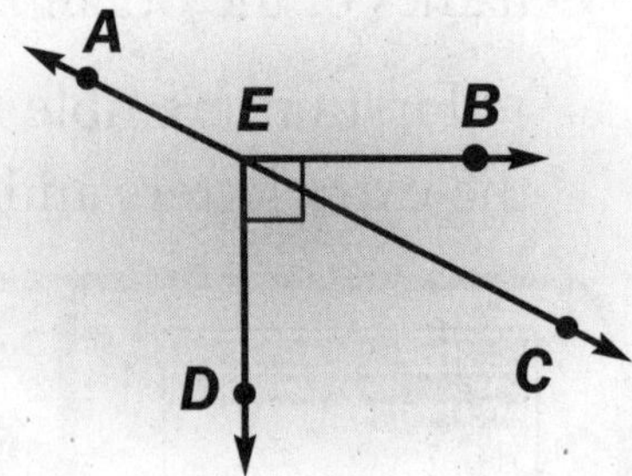

1. all acute angles ______________________

2. all obtuse angles ______________________

3. all straight angles ______________________

4. all right angles ______________________

5. Tell how you know there are no skew lines in the diagram shown on this page.

____

6. In the box on the right, draw $\angle LMN$ with measure 40°. Label the angle with points *L*, *M*, and *N*.

For Exercises 7–10, complete the sentence.

7. A protractor is a tool used for measuring ______________________. Its units are called ______________________.

8. Two rays that form an angle have a common endpoint called the angle ______________________.

9. The measure of any obtuse angle is ______________________.

10. The measure of any acute angle is ______________________.

Multiple Choice Choose one of the following terms to describe each object: *point*, *ray*, *line segment*, and *plane*.

11. short piece of wire ______________________ **12.** tip of a needle ______________________

13. football field ______________________ **14.** beam of light ______________________

Name ______________________

FOR USE WITH PAGE 184

Develop Language

A. Definition Chart Complete the Definition Chart below. Define each term and give an example.

Term	Definition	Sample Diagram
parallel lines		
intersecting lines		
line segment		
angle		
perpendicular lines		

B. Classifying Measure each angle with a protractor. Then write the angle and its measure in the correct column of the table to classify it as acute, right, or obtuse. $\angle A$ is done for you.

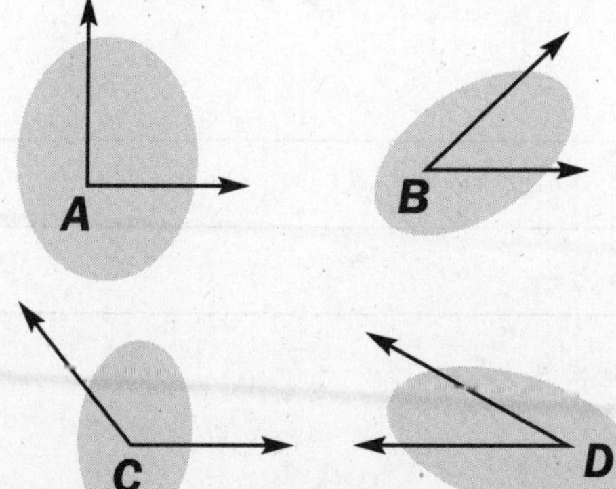

acute	right	obtuse
	90º, $\angle A$	

Name

Angles and Triangles

Practice

For Exercises 1–8, use the diagram on the right.

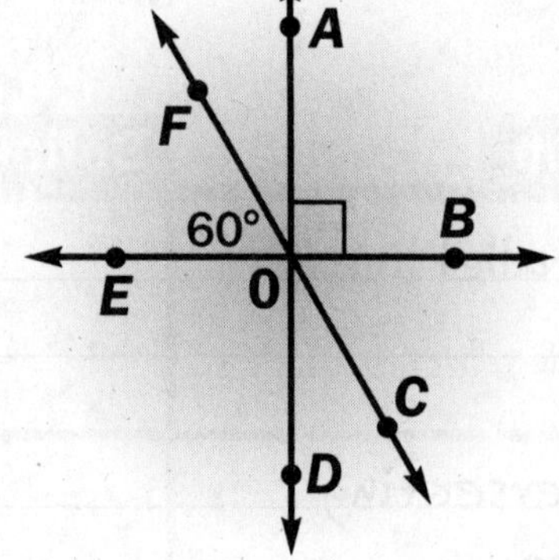

1. Name two pairs of vertical angles.

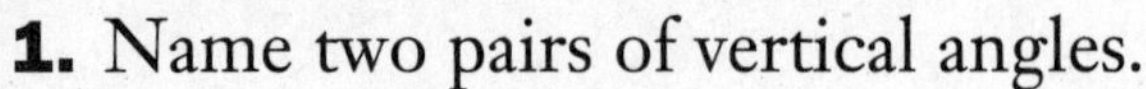

____

2. Name two pairs of complementary angles.

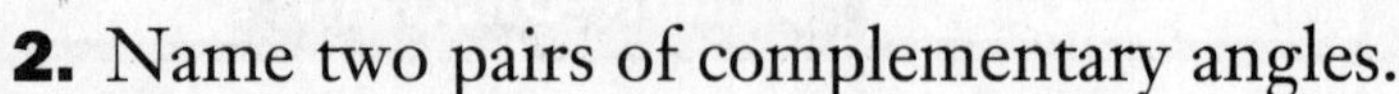

____

3. Name two pairs of supplementary angles.

____

Find the measure of each angle.

4. $\angle AOB$ ________ **5.** $\angle FOA$ ________ **6.** $\angle FOB$ ________

7. $\angle DOC$ ________ **8.** $\angle AOD$ ________

For Exercises 9–11, find each missing angle measure. Then classify each triangle as *acute*, *right*, or *obtuse*.

9.

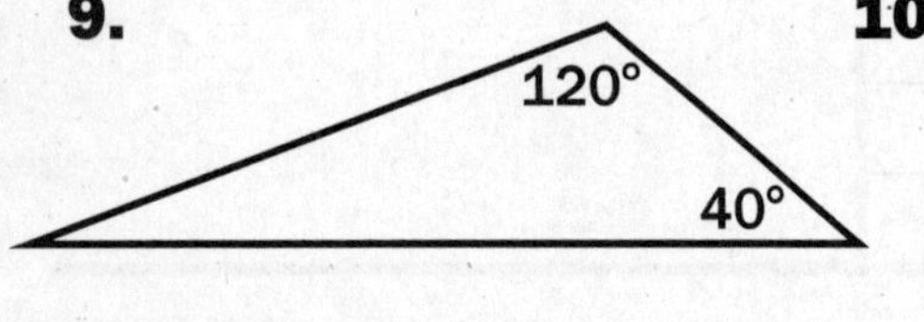

____

10.

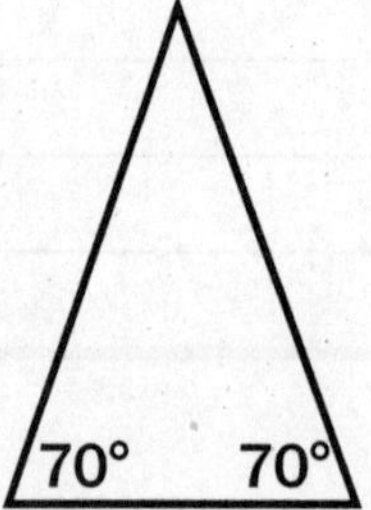

____

11.

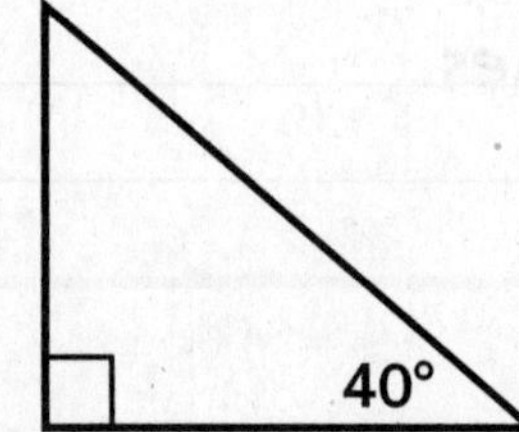

____

12. **Short Response** Can an obtuse triangle have a right angle? Why or why not?

____

____

____

Name ________________________________

FOR USE WITH PAGE 189

Develop Language

A. Define and Draw For each angle pair listed in the Word Band, give a definition and draw an example.

Word Bank
- complementary angles
- congruent angles
- supplementary angles
- vertical angles

a. congruent angles ________________
____

b. complementary angles ________________
____

c. supplementary angles ________________
____

d. vertical angles ________________
____

B. Describing For each term, complete the chart below. Include characteristics and diagrams of an example and a nonexample.

1. obtuse isosceles triangle

Definition	Characteristics
Example	**Nonexample**

2. right scalene triangle

Definition	Characteristics
Example	**Nonexample**

Name ______________________

Polygons

Practice

For Exercises 1–11, use the figures on the right. Give the letter of each figure. Some figures may have several letters.

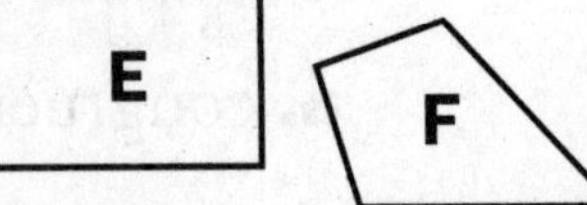

1. triangle ________ **2.** quadrilateral ________

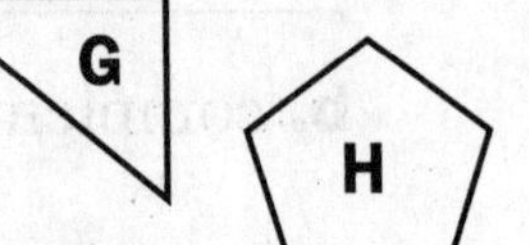

3. pentagon ________ **4.** hexagon ________

5. octagon ________ **6.** regular triangle ________

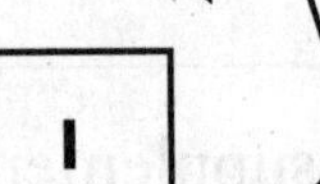

7. square ________ **8.** rhombus ________

9. trapezoid ________ **10.** rectangle ________

11. regular quadrilateral ________

12. **Short Response** Find the missing angle measure in trapezoid $ABCD$. Explain how you did it.

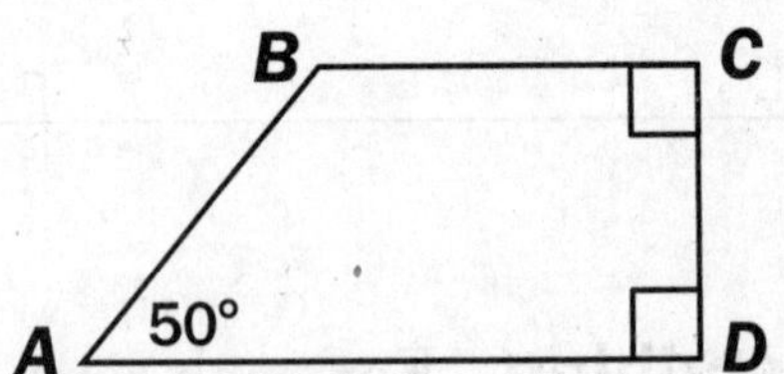

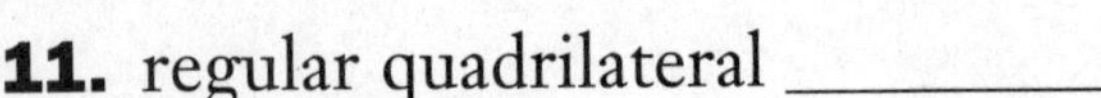

____

____

For Exercises 13 and 14, tell whether each sentence is always true, sometimes true, or never true.

13. Every rhombus is a square. ________

14. Every square is a rhombus. ________

15. **Short Response** What is the sum of the measures of the angles in any rectangle? Explain how you know.

____

____

____

Name ______________________

FOR USE WITH PAGE 194

Develop Language

A. Definition Chart Complete the Definition Chart below. Define each term and give an example.

Term	Definition	Sample Diagram
parallelogram		
trapezoid		
rectangle		
rhombus		
square		

B. Synthesizing Synthesize the information you learned about triangles by completing the table below. Draw and measure the triangles as needed.

Triangle	Number of ≅ Sides	Number of ≅ Angles	Number of Right Angles
right scalene			
right isosceles			
acute scalene			
acute isosceles			
obtuse scalene			
obtuse isosceles			
equilateral			

Name

Congruent Figures

Practice

For Exercises 1 and 2, use the figures on the right.

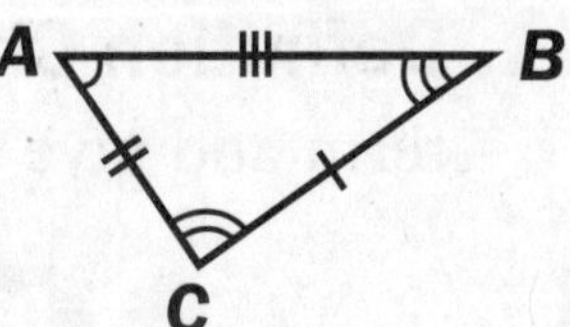

1. Name all pairs of congruent angles.

___

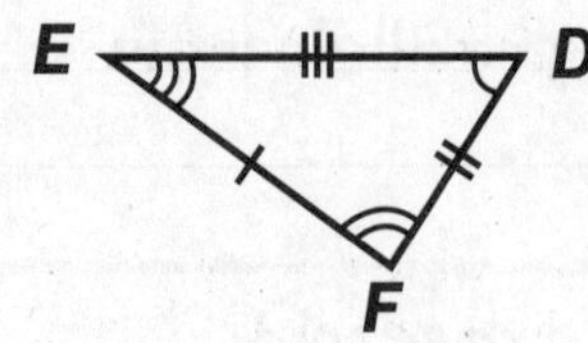

2. Name all pairs of congruent sides.

___

3. Quadrilaterals MATH and WORK are congruent.
List all pairs of corresponding sides and corresponding angles.

Sides: ___

Angles: ___

For Exercises 4 and 5, find each missing measure.

4.

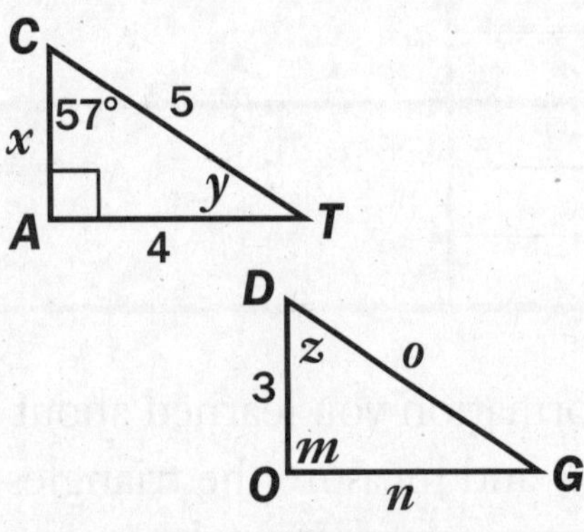

$\triangle CAT \cong \triangle DOG$

x ___ y ___ z ___

m ___ n ___ o ___

5.

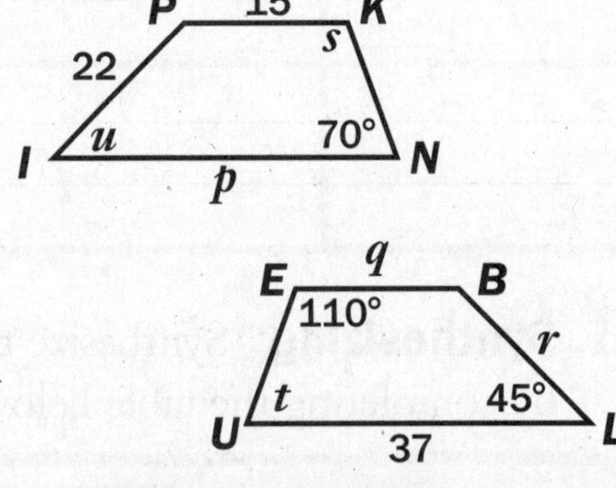

$PINK \cong BLUE$

p ___ q ___ r ___

s ___ t ___ u ___

6. **Extended Response** Tell in your own words what it means for two figures to be congruent. Then draw a pair of congruent figures.

___

___

___

Name ________________________

FOR USE WITH PAGE 199

Develop Language

A. Web Complete the Web on the right. Then use a centimeter ruler and protractor to draw $\triangle FGH$ congruent to $\triangle KLM$ below. Explain how you drew $\triangle FGH$.

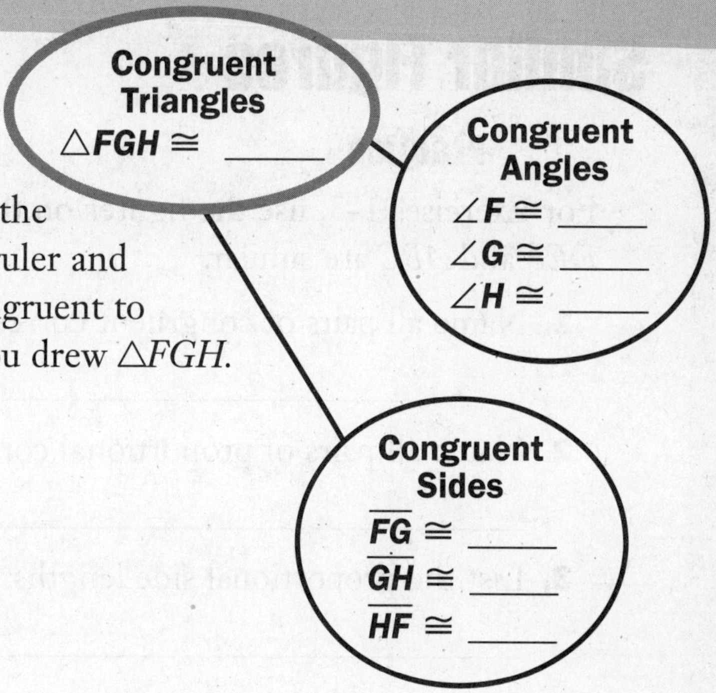

Congruent Triangles
$\triangle FGH \cong$ ______

Congruent Angles
$\angle F \cong$ ______
$\angle G \cong$ ______
$\angle H \cong$ ______

Congruent Sides
$\overline{FG} \cong$ ______
$\overline{GH} \cong$ ______
$\overline{HF} \cong$ ______

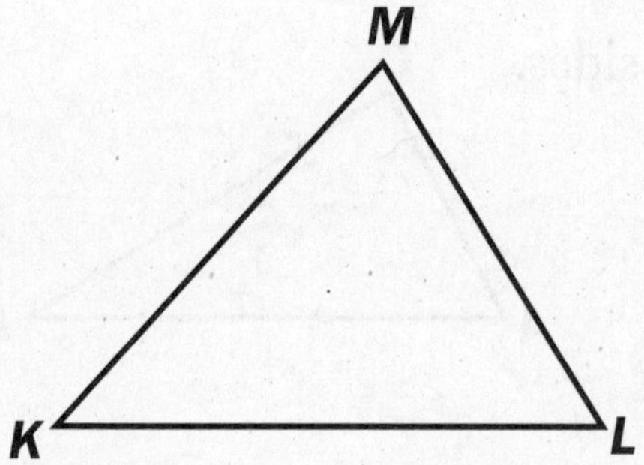

M

K L

____

____

____

____

B. Summarizing Summarize what you know about congruent figures by drawing two congruent trapezoids. Label the trapezoids *ABCD* and *EFGH*. Then fill in the table listing all pairs of congruent sides and congruent angles. Also measure the sides and angles.

ABCD *EFGH*

Pairs of ≅ Sides	Pairs of ≅ Angles

Name

Similar Figures

Practice

For Exercises 1–3, use the figures on the right. Triangles *DEF* and *ABC* are similar.

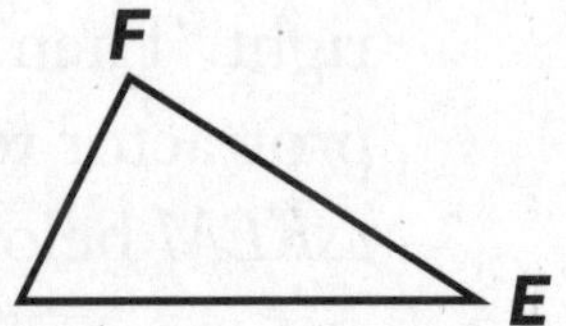

1. Name all pairs of congruent corresponding angles.

____

2. Name all pairs of proportional corresponding sides.

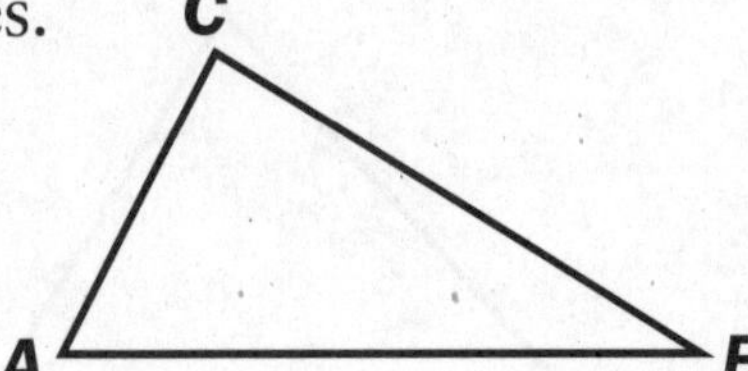

____

3. List the proportional side lengths.

____

For Exercises 4 and 5, find each missing measure.

4.

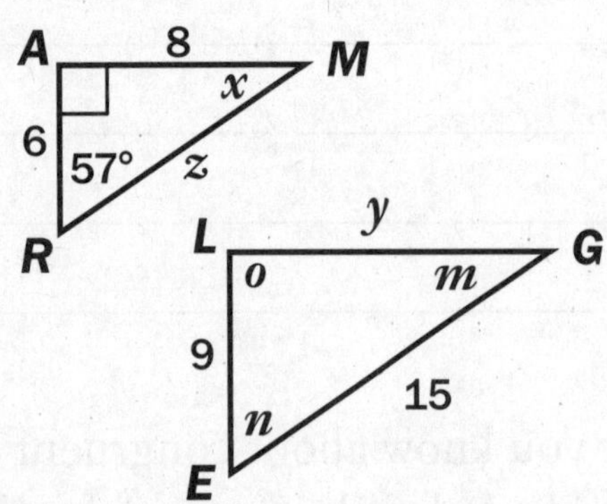

$\triangle ARM \sim \triangle LEG$

x _____ *y* _____ *z* _____

m _____ *n* _____ *o* _____

5.

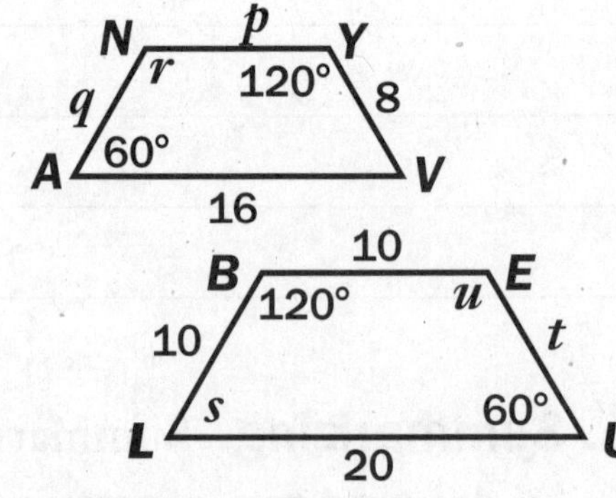

NAVY ~ *BLUE*

p _____ *q* _____ *r* _____

s _____ *t* _____ *u* _____

6. **Extended Response** List the dimensions of three rectangles similar to a rectangle that is 9 in. by 12 in. At least one of the rectangles should be smaller. Explain how you found the dimensions.

____

____

____

____

Name

FOR USE WITH PAGE 204

Develop Language

A. Measure and Draw Use an inch ruler and a protractor to draw $\triangle FGH$ similar to $\triangle KLM$ below. Use the proportion $\frac{FG}{KL} = \frac{3}{4}$. Explain how you drew $\triangle FGH$. Include the vocabulary words *similar*, *proportional*, *corresponding*, and *ratio*.

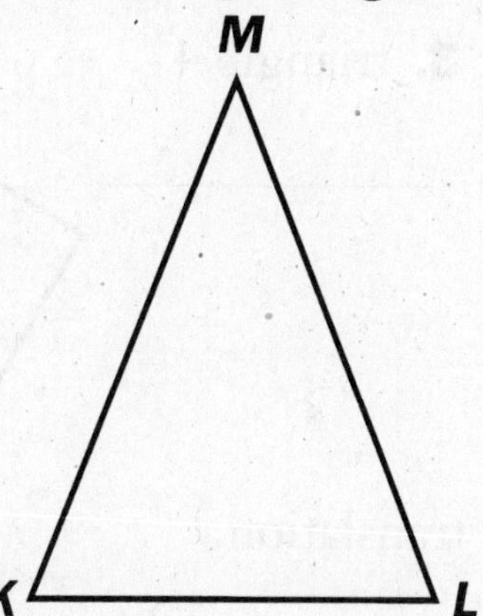

B. Identifying You can identify properties of kites by measuring the sides and angles of a number of them. Measure the sides and angles of the kites on the right. Then write a list of their properties. One property has been given for you.

Two pairs of sides are congruent.

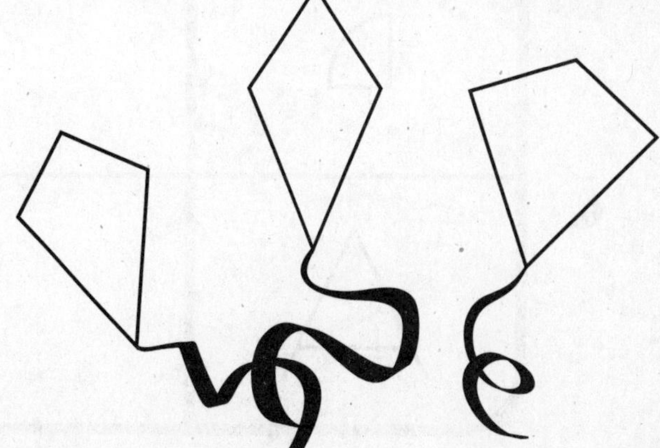

Name

Transformations

Practice

For Exercises 1–3, use the diagram on the right. Triangle 1 is the pre-image and triangles 2, 3, and 4 are the images. Tell whether each image is a translation, reflection, or rotation of triangle 1.

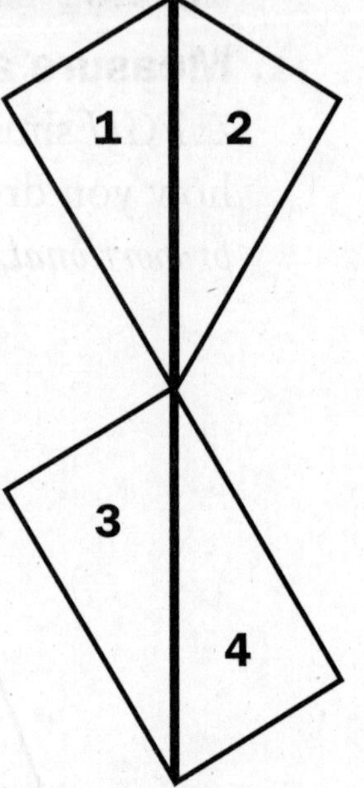

1. triangle 2 **2.** triangle 3 **3.** triangle 4

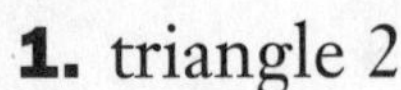

For each figure in Exercises 4–6, draw a translation, a reflection, and a rotation.

	Translation	Reflection	Rotation
4.			
5.			
6.			

Name ____________________

FOR USE WITH PAGE 209

Develop Language

A. Match Match each definition with the correct term. Use each definition only once.

_____ transformation	**a.** a change in position by turning
_____ translation	**b.** a design of repeating shapes that fit together with no spaces between them
_____ reflection	**c.** a change in position of a figure
_____ rotation	**d.** a change in position by flipping
_____ tessellation	**e.** a change in position by sliding

B. Explaining Look at the pattern on the right. Explain how each transformation was created. If it helps, you can trace the picture and cut out the figures.

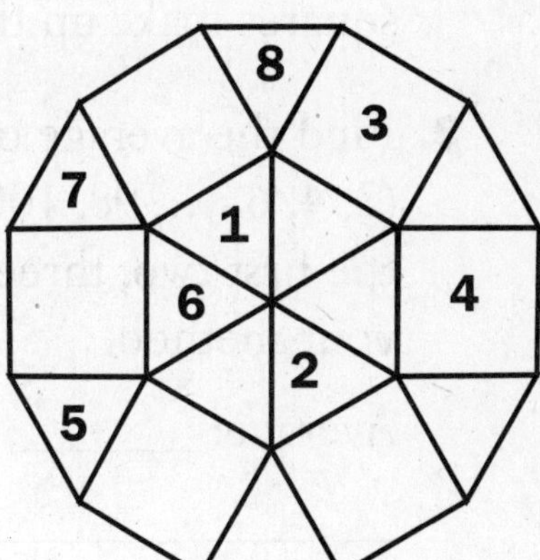

1. Figure 1 to figure 2

____

2. Figure 3 to figure 4

____

3. Figure 5 to figure 6

____

4. Figure 7 to figure 8

____.

Name

Problem Solving

Problem-Solving Skills

- Draw a Diagram
- Guess, Check, and Revise
- Look for a Pattern
- Make an Organized List
- Make a Model
- Make a Table
- Simulate a Problem
- **Solve a Simpler Problem**
- Use Logical Reasoning
- Work Backward
- Write an Equation

Solve a Simpler Problem

Solve these problems by *solving a simpler problem* first. Then use that same method to solve each problem.

1. Each triangle in the diagram is an equilateral triangle. Every side of the equilateral triangle measures 2 meters. What is the distance around the outside of a parallelogram formed:

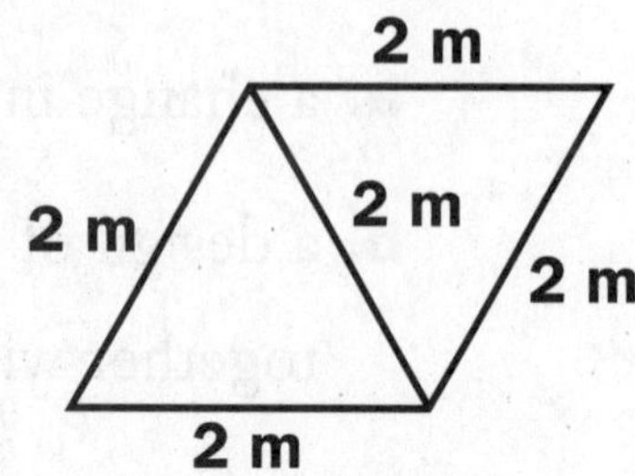

By 2 triangles? ______ By 10 triangles? ______

By 100 triangles? ______

2. Examine the picture on the right. How many small squares make up the cube's six faces? ______

3. Find the average of the even numbers 2 through 100 (2, 4, 6, ..., 98, 100). Start by finding the average of the first two, three, and four even numbers. Explain your method.

Average: ______; ______

______

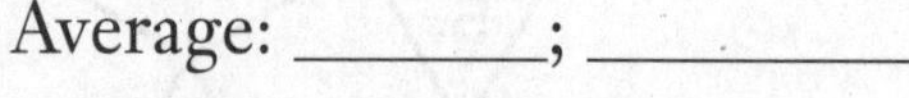

My Summary of the Unit

______
______
______
______
______
______
______
______

Name

FOR USE WITH PAGES 180–211

Unit Vocabulary

A. Tangrams The game of tangrams is several thousand years old. People created pictures with the pieces below and made up stories about them. To create a tangram picture, you must use all seven polygons and arrange them to form a shape. The pieces must touch but not overlap. Identify each of the seven polygons. Tell which are congruent.

B. More Tangrams Trace and then cut out the polygons. Use all seven of them to form each of the three black shapes shown below. Use each polygon only once. Then create your own tangram shape and tell a story about it.

Perimeter and Area

Practice

For Exercises 1–3, find the perimeter and area of each figure.

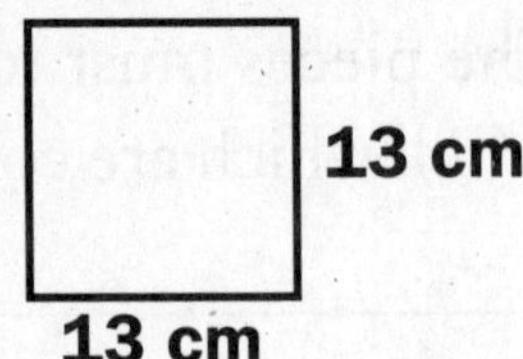

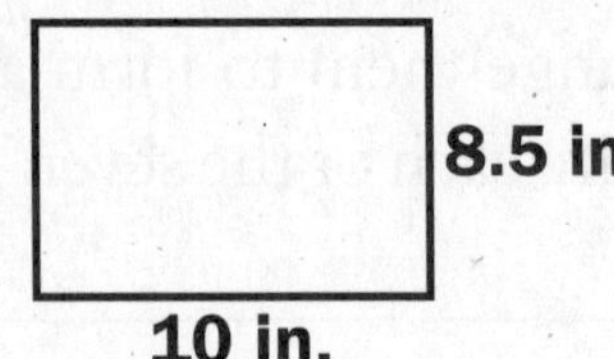

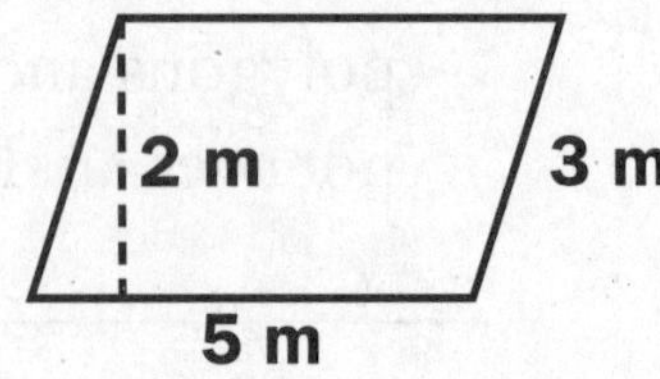

1. ____________ **2.** ____________ **3.** ____________

For Exercises 4 and 5, use the diagram on the right.

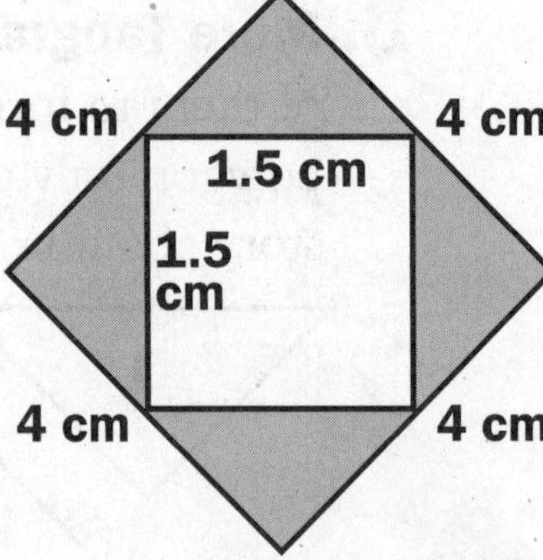

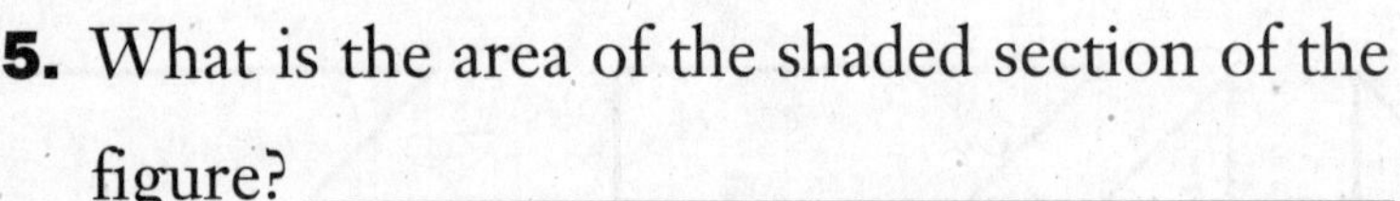

4. What is the perimeter of the unshaded square in the middle of the figure? ____________

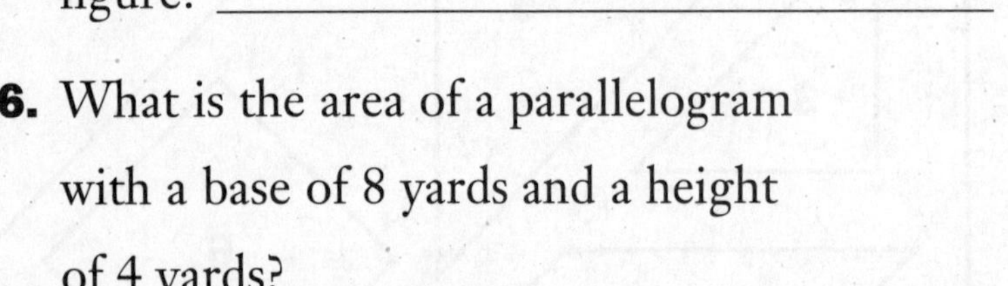

5. What is the area of the shaded section of the figure? ____________

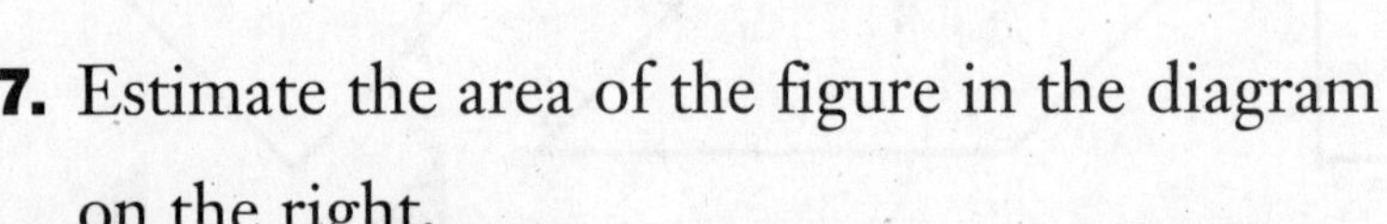

6. What is the area of a parallelogram with a base of 8 yards and a height of 4 yards? ____________

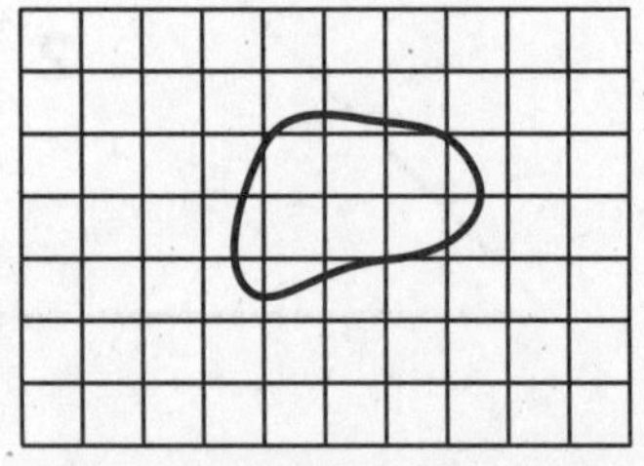

7. Estimate the area of the figure in the diagram on the right. ____________

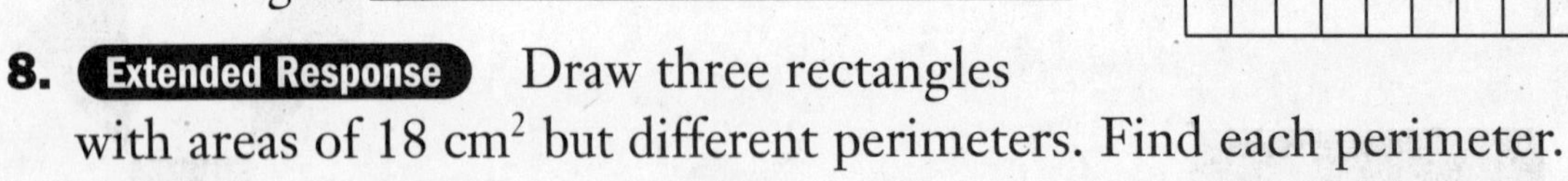

8. **Extended Response** Draw three rectangles with areas of 18 cm^2 but different perimeters. Find each perimeter.

Name ______________________

FOR USE WITH PAGE 216

Develop Language

A. Venn Diagram Complete the Venn Diagram below to compare and contrast area and perimeter.

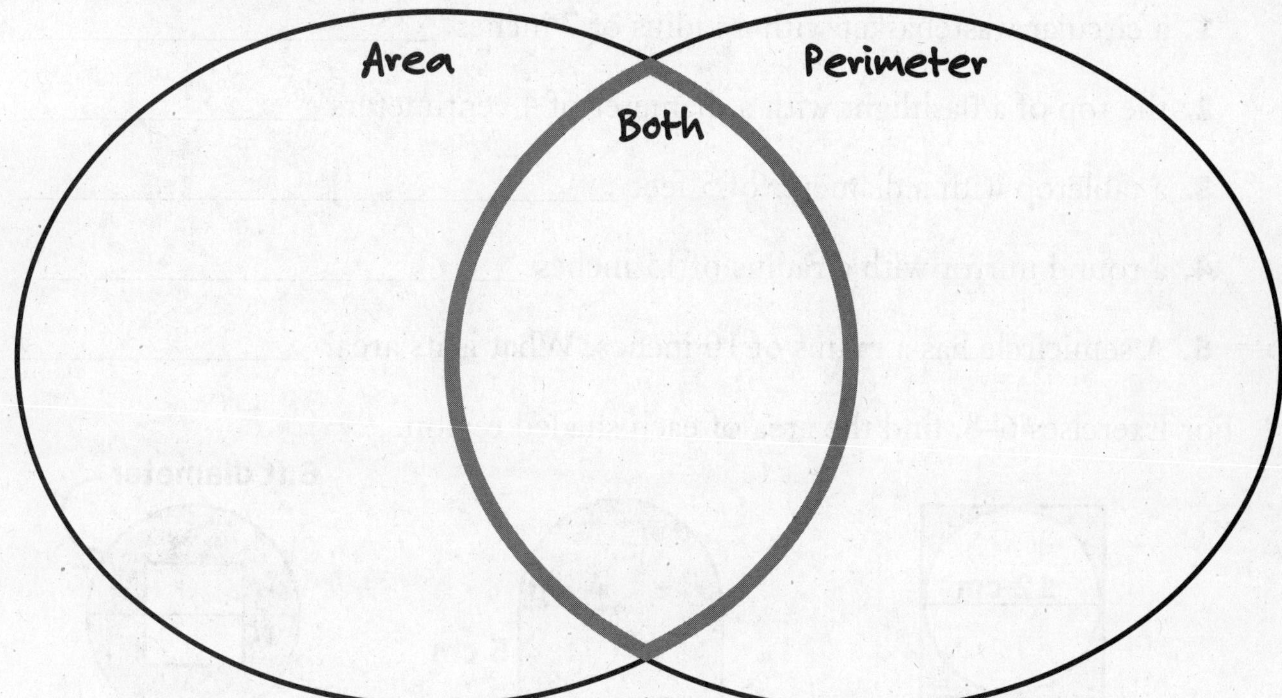

B. Connecting Paul has enough material to make a fence 22 feet long. He will use this material to fence off a rectangular section of his yard. The rectangle's sides must all be whole numbers. Think about the connection between perimeter and area to answer the following questions. Use square tiles, grid paper, or other materials to help.

1. What is the greatest area that he can enclose with his fence? How do you know it is the greatest area? ______________________

____

____

2. What is the least area he can enclose with his fence? How do you know it is the least? ______________________

____

Name

Circles

Practice

For Exercises 1–4, find the circumference of each object. Use 3.14 for pi and round answers to the nearest tenth.

1. a circular wastebasket with a radius of 7 inches ____________

2. the top of a flashlight with a diameter of 4 centimeters ____________

3. a tabletop with a diameter of 5 feet ____________

4. a round mirror with a radius of 15 inches ____________

5. A semicircle has a radius of 10 inches. What is its area? ____________

For Exercises 6–8, find the area of each shaded region.

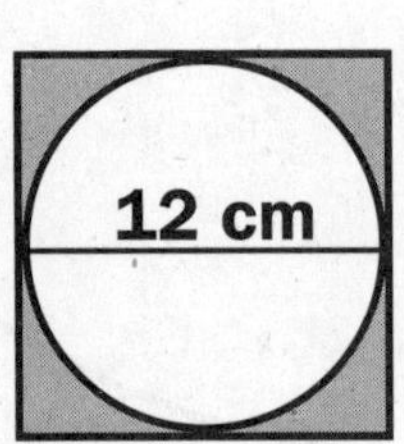

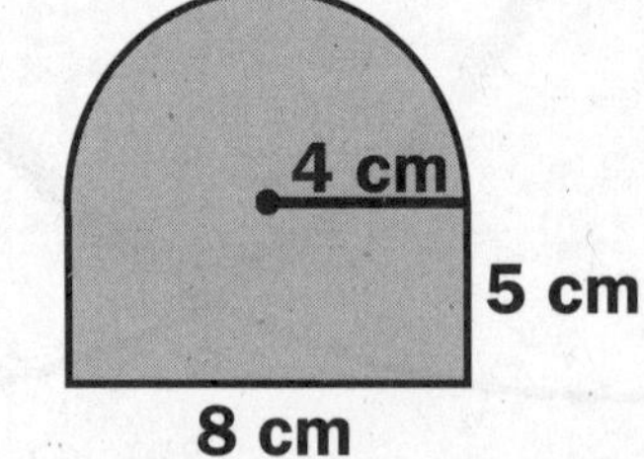

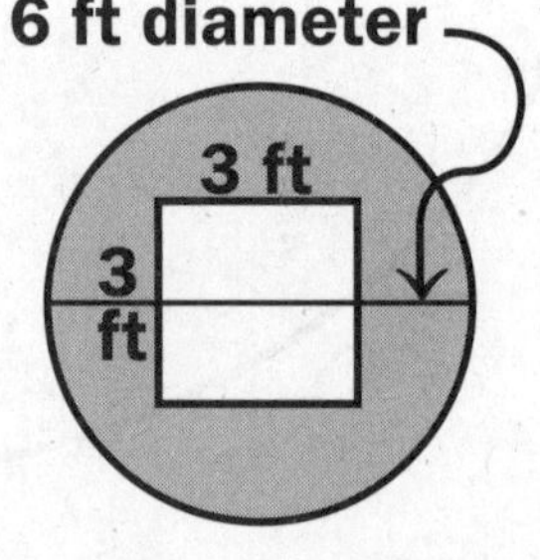

6. ____________ **7.** ____________ **8.** ____________

9. Complete each sentence: As the diameter of a circle increases, the circumference of the circle ____________. As the radius of a circle decreases, the area of the circle ____________.

10. **Short Response** Lucia says that if she knows the circumference of a circular dinner plate, she can figure out the plate's diameter and area. Do you agree or disagree? Explain.

____

____

____

Name

FOR USE WITH PAGE 221

Develop Language

A. Fill In Complete the organizers below. In the empty boxes, write or draw what you know about the words *radius* and *diameter.* Then write a sentence that shows how the two words are related.

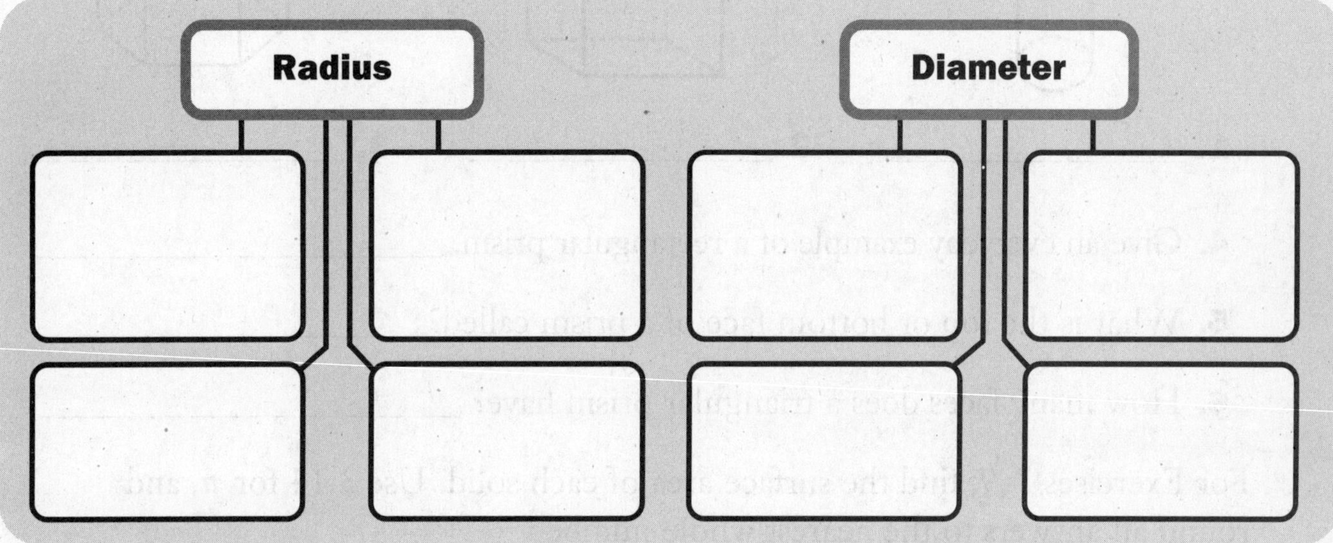

B. Organizing Organize what you know about the words *pi* and *circumference* by completing an organizer for each. Then write a sentence that shows how the two words are related.

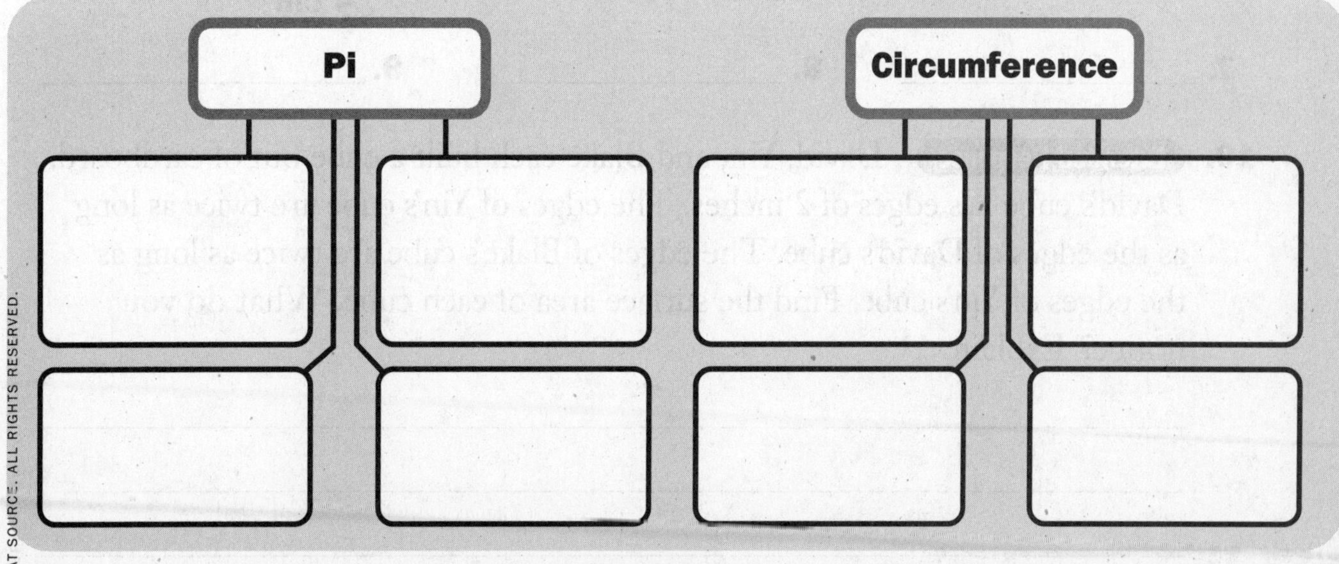

Surface Area

Practice

For Exercises 1–3, name each solid.

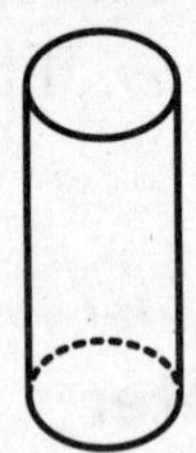

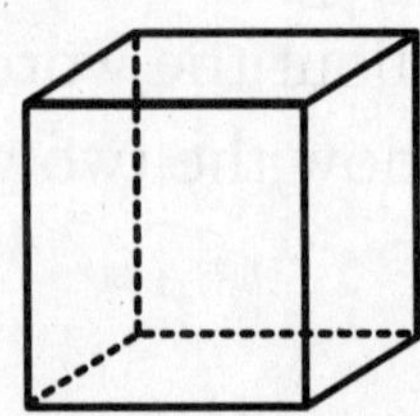

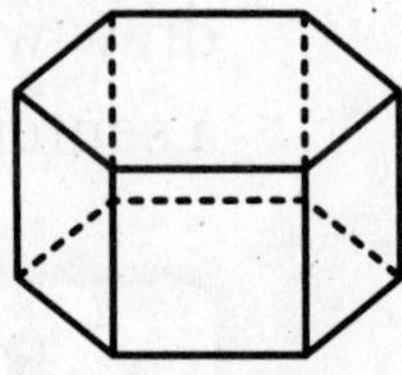

1. ____________ **2.** ____________ **3.** ____________

4. Give an everyday example of a rectangular prism. ____________

5. What is the top or bottom face of a prism called? ____________

6. How many faces does a triangular prism have? ____________

For Exercises 7–9, find the surface area of each solid. Use 3.14 for π, and round all answers to the nearest whole number.

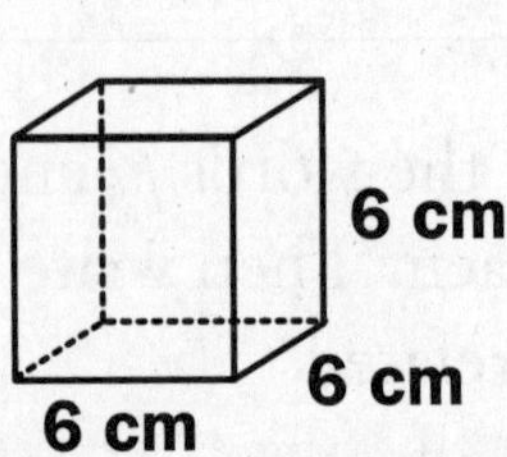

3 in.
5 in.

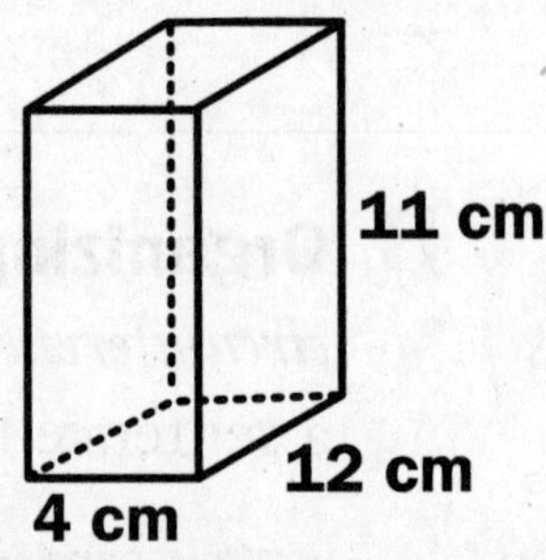

7. ____________ **8.** ____________ **9.** ____________

10. **Extended Response** David, Yin, and Blake each built a cube out of cardboard. David's cube has edges of 2 inches. The edges of Yin's cube are twice as long as the edges of David's cube. The edges of Blake's cube are twice as long as the edges of Yin's cube. Find the surface area of each cube. What do you notice? Explain.

Name

FOR USE WITH PAGE 226

Develop Language

A. Sequence Notes Complete the Sequence Notes below to tell how to find the surface area of the rectangular prism shown. You may draw extra boxes if you need them.

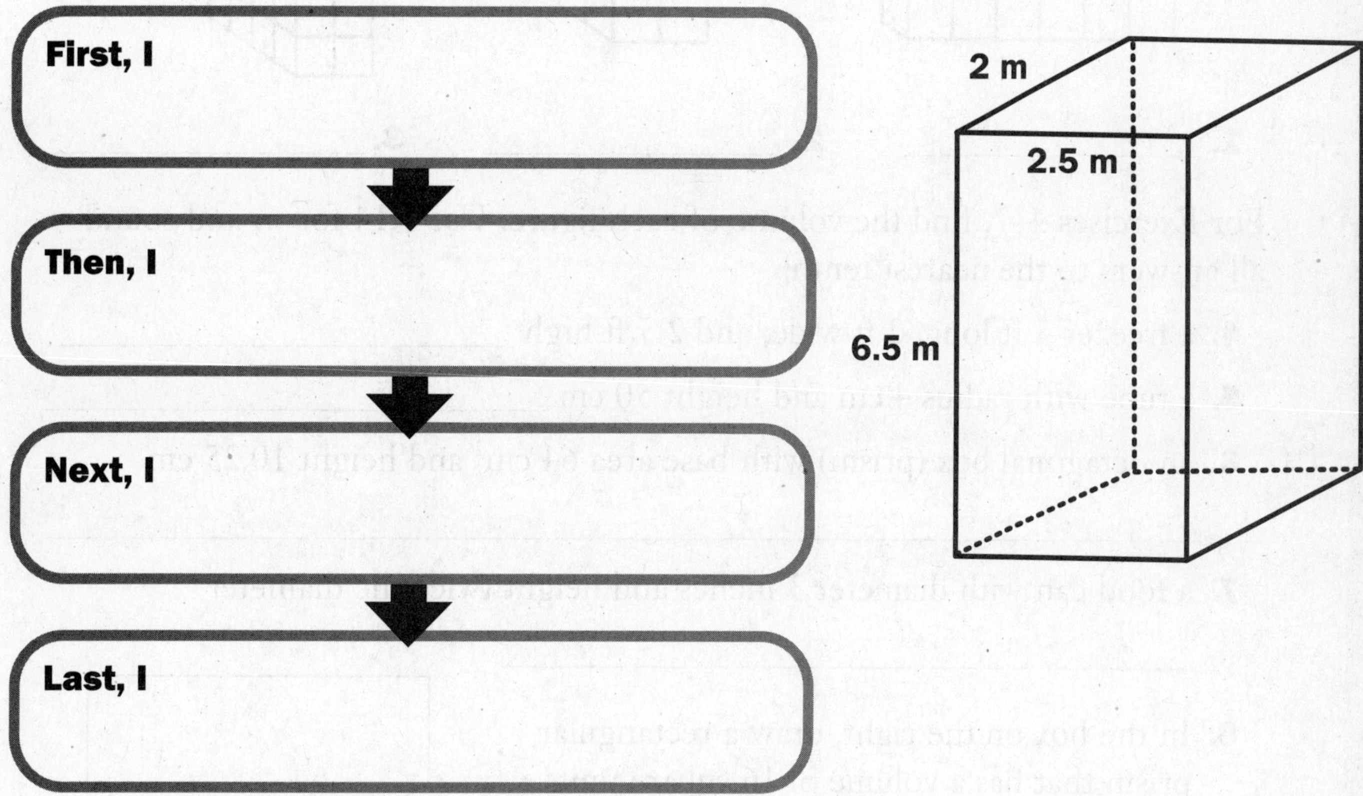

B. Persuading Elaine has two gift boxes. Each box is a rectangular prism. The first box is 7 cm × 9 cm × 3 cm. The second box is 6 cm × 8 cm × 5 cm. Elaine has 230 cm^2 of wrapping paper. Does it matter which box she uses? After answering the question, persuade Elaine that you are right by describing what you did.

Name

FOR USE WITH PAGES 227–230

Volume

Practice

For Exercises 1–3, count the cubes to find the volume of each rectangular prism.

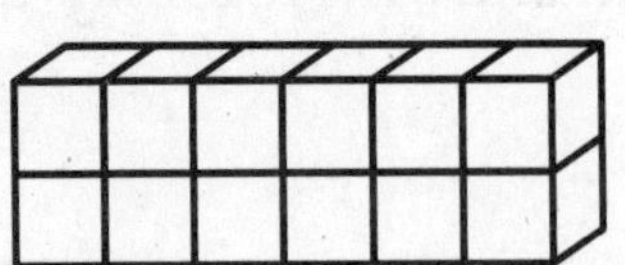

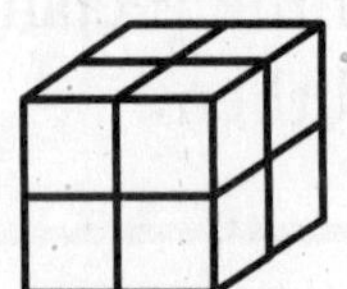

1. ______ **2.** ______ **3.** ______

For Exercises 4–7, find the volume of each figure. Use 3.14 for π, and round all answers to the nearest tenth.

4. a freezer 5 ft long, 2 ft wide, and 2.5 ft high ______

5. a tube with radius 4 cm and height 50 cm ______

6. an octagonal box (prism) with base area 64 cm^2 and height 10.25 cm

______

7. a food can with diameter 3 inches and height twice the diameter

______

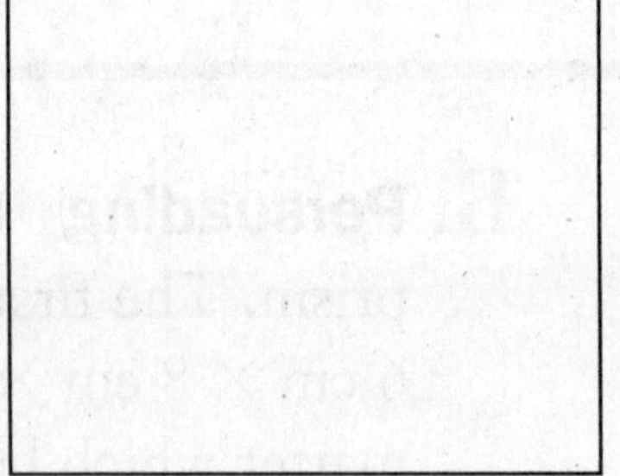

8. In the box on the right, draw a rectangular prism that has a volume of 16 square units.

9. A can of liquid has a height of 7.5 inches and a top with a radius of 2 inches. If the can is half full, what is the volume of the liquid inside?

______

10. **Extended Response** Ms. Park made 60 wooden blocks. Each block is a cube with side length 1 inch. She wants to put the blocks into a rectangular box that measures 7 inches long, 4 inches wide, and 2 inches high. Is the box large enough to hold all the blocks? Explain.

______

______

Name ....

FOR USE WITH PAGE 231

Develop Language

A. Web Complete the Web below. Write words or numbers in the ovals to tell what you know about volume.

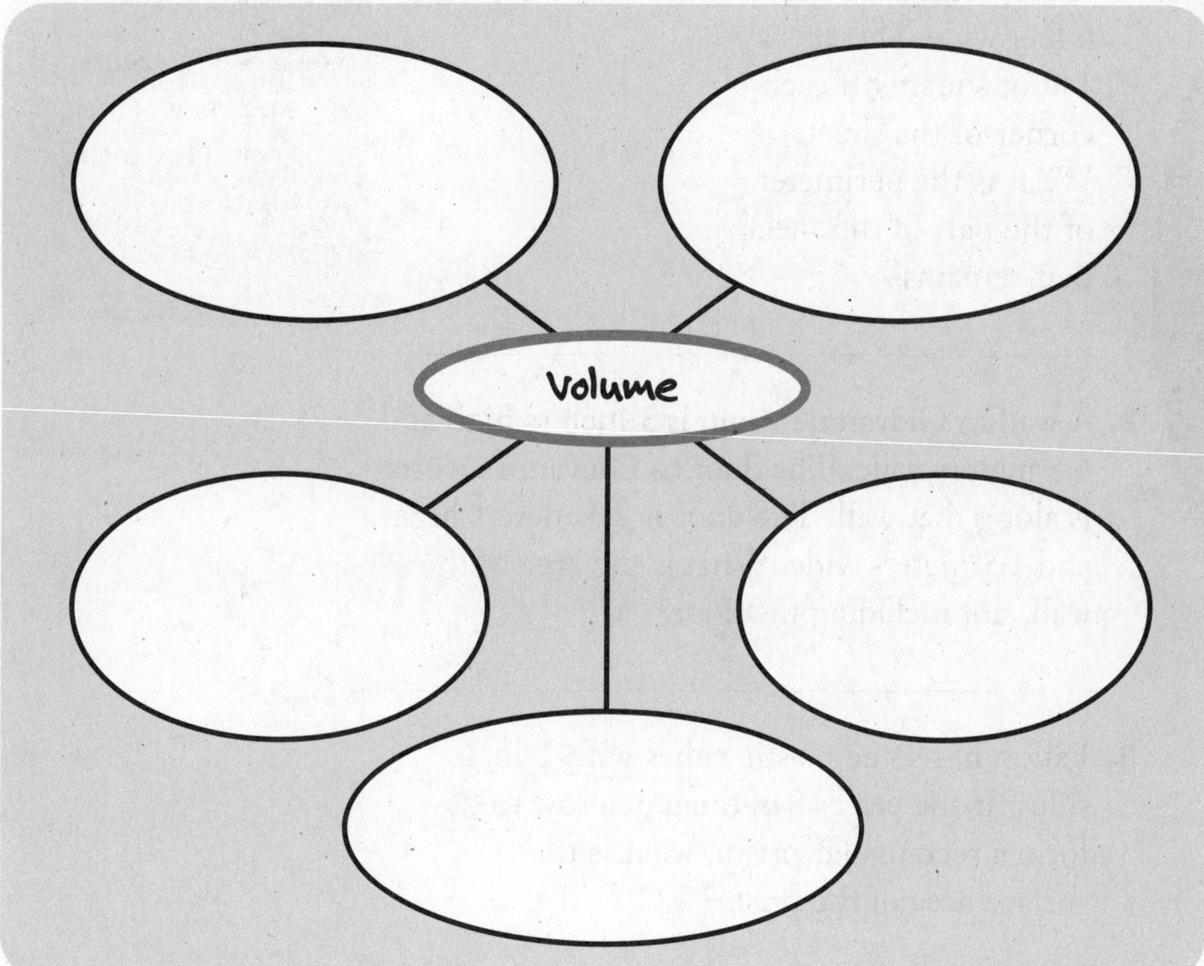

B. Comparing and Contrasting The list on the right gives four different measures you have learned to find. Choose two of the measures. Then write two sentences telling how the measures are alike and how they are different.

1. Perimeter of a rectangle
2. Area of a rectangle
3. Surface area of a rectangular prism
4. Volume of a rectangular prism

____

____

____

Name

Problem Solving

Problem-Solving Skills

- Draw a Diagram
- Guess, Check, and Revise
- Look for a Pattern
- Make an Organized List
- Make a Model
- Make a Table
- Simulate a Problem
- Solve a Simpler Problem
- Use Logical Reasoning
- Work Backward
- Write an Equation

Draw a Diagram

Draw a diagram to help you solve these problems.

1. Mai Li has an old bed sheet 8 feet long and 6 feet wide. She cuts a 1-foot square off each corner of the sheet. What is the perimeter of the part of the sheet that remains?

____

2. A wall in Giovanni's room is 3 meters high and 4.5 meters wide. The door to Giovanni's closet is along that wall. The door is 2.5 meters high and 1.5 meters wide. What is the area of the wall, not including the door?

____

3. Fallon has some plastic cubes with 1-inch sides. If she places 8 of them in a row to form a rectangular prism, what is the surface area of the prism?

____

My Summary of the Unit

Name ____________________

Unit Vocabulary

Sentence Frames Read the sentences. Fill in the blanks with terms so that the sentences make sense. Use the Word Bank at the bottom of the page.

1. To find the ________________ of a ________________, multiply the diameter by pi.

2. To find the ________________ of a ________________, multiply the length by the width.

3. To find the ________________ of a ________________, multiply its length, its width, and its height all together.

4. To find the ________________ of a ________________, multiply the length of any of its sides by 4.

5. To find the ________________ of a ________________, add the area of the bases to the area of the curved rectangle.

6. A ________________ is a prism with equal measures for its length, width, and height.

7. To find the area of a base of a cylinder, you need to know the ________________ of the base.

Word Bank

area	cube
surface area	perimeter
rectangle	radius
volume	circle
square	cylinder
circumference	prism

Name ______________________

What Is Probability?

Practice

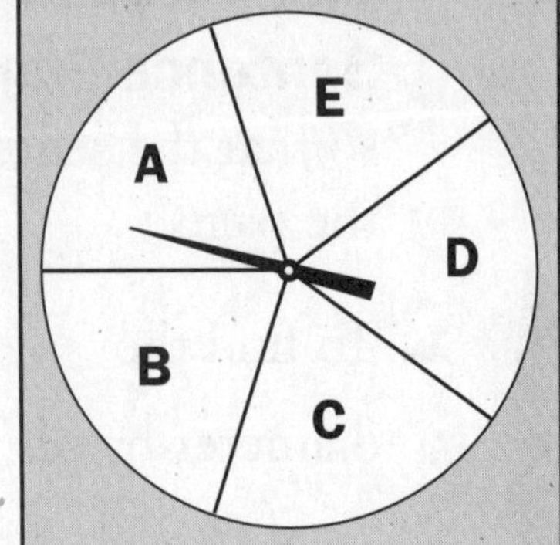

For Exercises 1–3, use the spinner.

1. How many ways are there to spin a consonant? ______________________

2. What is the probability of spinning D? __________

3. What is the probability of spinning a vowel? ____

For Exercises 4–6, use a number cube labeled 1 through 6.

4. What is the probability of rolling 6? ______________________

5. What is the probability of rolling an odd number? ______________

6. What is the probability of *not* rolling 3? ______________________

For Exercises 7–9, imagine picking a numbered card out of a hat. The cards in the hat have the numbers 10, 20, 30, and 40.

7. Name an outcome that is certain (must happen). ______________________

8. Name an event that is impossible (cannot happen). ______________________

9. Name an outcome that is likely (might happen). ______________________

10. **Short Response** Spinner A has 10 equal sections, 6 of which are green. Spinner B has 8 equal sections, 5 of which are green. Which spinner has the greater probability of spinning green? Explain.

____

Name ______________________________

FOR USE WITH PAGE 238

Develop Language

A. Question and Answer Use Lesson 41 in *ACCESS Math* to help you complete the chart.

WHAT is probability?	WHEN do I use probability?	HOW do I measure probability?	WHY is probability important?

B. Interpreting Use two number cubes, each labeled 1 through 6. Roll both cubes, and record the sum of the two numbers in a frequency table. Repeat until you have rolled both number cubes 25 times. Finally, interpret the sums by calculating and comparing $P(1)$, $P(7)$, and $P(12)$. For a challenge, find the probability of rolling doubles, the same number on both cubes. Explain your results.

____

____

____

____

____

____

Name ____________________

Making Predictions

Practice

For Exercises 1–3, use the spinner.

1. What is the probability of spinning an odd number? ____________

2. What is the probability of spinning an even number? ____________

3. What is the sum of the probabilities in Exercises 1 and 2? Explain.

____

____

4. A soccer team has 5 wins, 3 losses, and 6 ties. What is the experimental probability that the team will win its next game? _____ What is the most likely outcome of the next game? Explain your reasoning. ____________

____

____

Extended Response Tamara is playing a game with number cubes. She rolls two cubes at a time. If both number cubes are odd, she wins. The table shows her results so far.

Both odd	6
One odd, one even	13
Both even	6

5. Find the experimental probability that Tamara will win the next round. Write it as a fraction, a decimal, and a percent.

____

6. Find the experimental probability that she will lose. Write it as a fraction, a decimal, and a percent.

____

Name

FOR USE WITH PAGE 243

Develop Language

A. Web Write important details about experimental probability in the Web below. Then write a sentence about experimental probability.

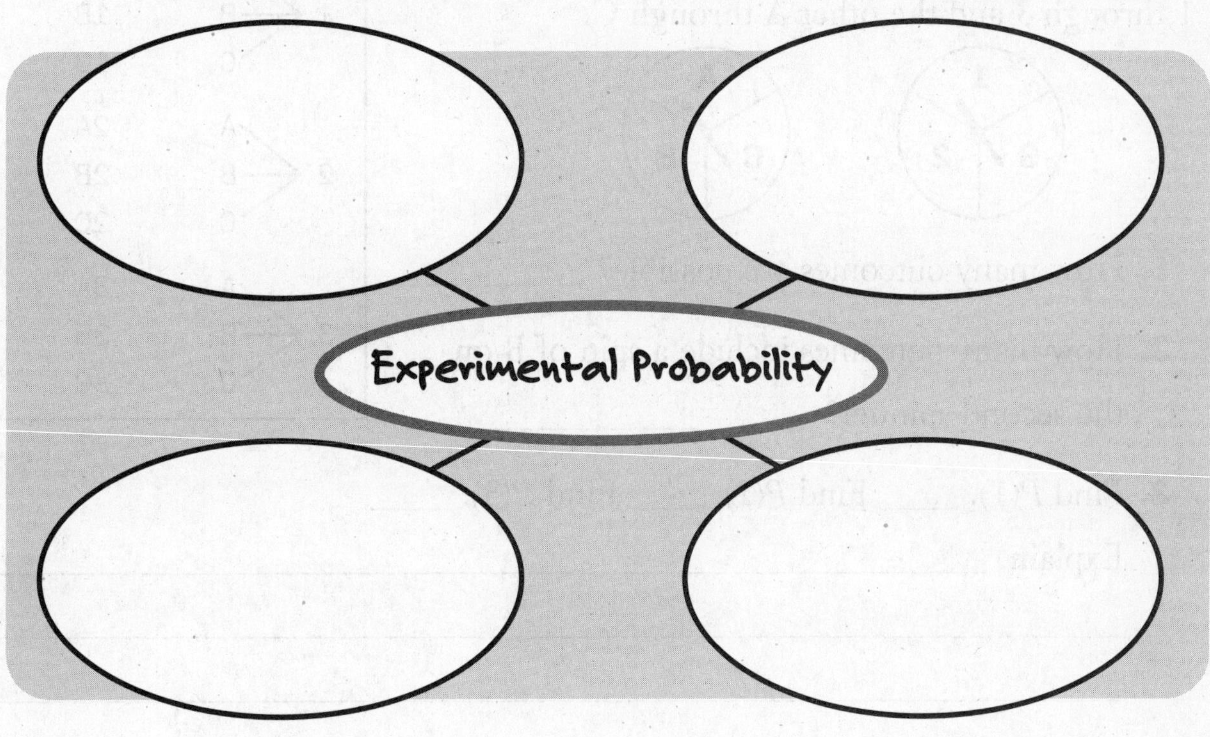

B. Predicting Put 4 red and 2 blue marbles into a hat. Predict the color of marble you would expect someone to draw out of the hat when drawing one marble. Now draw a marble, record the color, and put it back in the hat. Do this 15 times. Then find the experimental probabilities for $P(\text{red})$ and $P(\text{blue})$. Compare these results with your prediction.

Counting

Practice

For Exercises 1–4, use the tree diagram. It shows the outcomes of spinning two spinners, one labeled 1 through 3 and the other A through C.

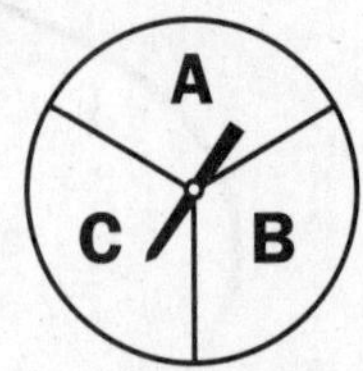

Tree Diagram

1st Spin	2nd Spin	Outcome
1	A	1A
	B	1B
	C	1C
2	A	2A
	B	2B
	C	2C
3	A	3A
	B	3B
	C	3C

1. How many outcomes are possible? ____________

2. How many outcomes include a spin of B on the second spinner? ____________

3. Find $P(1)$. ____ Find $P(2)$. ____ Find $P(3)$. ____

Explain. ____________

____

____

4. What is $P(2A)$? ____________

5. A class spends the day at the park. First, students must choose hiking or swimming. Then they choose to play basketball, soccer, or softball. Use the counting principle to find how many combinations of two activities are possible.

____

6. **Multiple Choice** The high school choir has 3 sopranos, 4 altos, 2 tenors, and 5 basses. The choir director will choose one singer from each voice part to form a quartet. Use the counting principle to find how many ways the choir director can do this.

A. 4 **B.** 9 **C.** 14 **D.** 120

Name

FOR USE WITH PAGE 248

Develop Language

A. Definition Chart Complete the Definition Chart below. Define each term and give an example.

Term	Definition	Example
compound event		
counting principle		
tree diagram		

B. Persuading At Gus's Sandwich Shop, you can choose from 5 sandwiches, 3 salads, and 3 soups. At Grand Deli, you can choose from 8 sandwiches, 2 salads, and 2 soups. Which store offers more combinations of a sandwich, a salad, and a bowl of soup? Write a sentence to persuade a friend that your answer is correct.

Name

Arrangements

Practice

For Exercises 1–3, write *yes* or *no* to tell if order matters. Explain your answer.

1. Calling a 7-digit telephone number ______

______

2. Choosing 2 books from a shelf ______

______

3. Lining up 3 children from shortest to tallest ______

______

4. Three friends go for a bicycle ride. They ride in single file. In how many different orders can the riders be arranged? ______

5. How many 3-letter permutations can be made from the letters A, B, C, D? ______ How many 2-letter permutations? ______ How many 2-letter permutations that do not include a vowel?

______

6. Four students want to be on the library committee. How many combinations of two students can Ms. Alvarez choose from these four?

______

7. **Extended Response** Read the two situations carefully. Tell how they are different. Then solve each problem.

Ms. Ayn has 5 CDs. In how many ways can she choose two CDs to donate?	Mr. Johns has 5 CDs. In how many orders can he play the CDs?

Name

FOR USE WITH PAGE 253

Develop Language

A. Venn Diagram Complete the Venn Diagram below. Compare and contrast combinations and permutations.

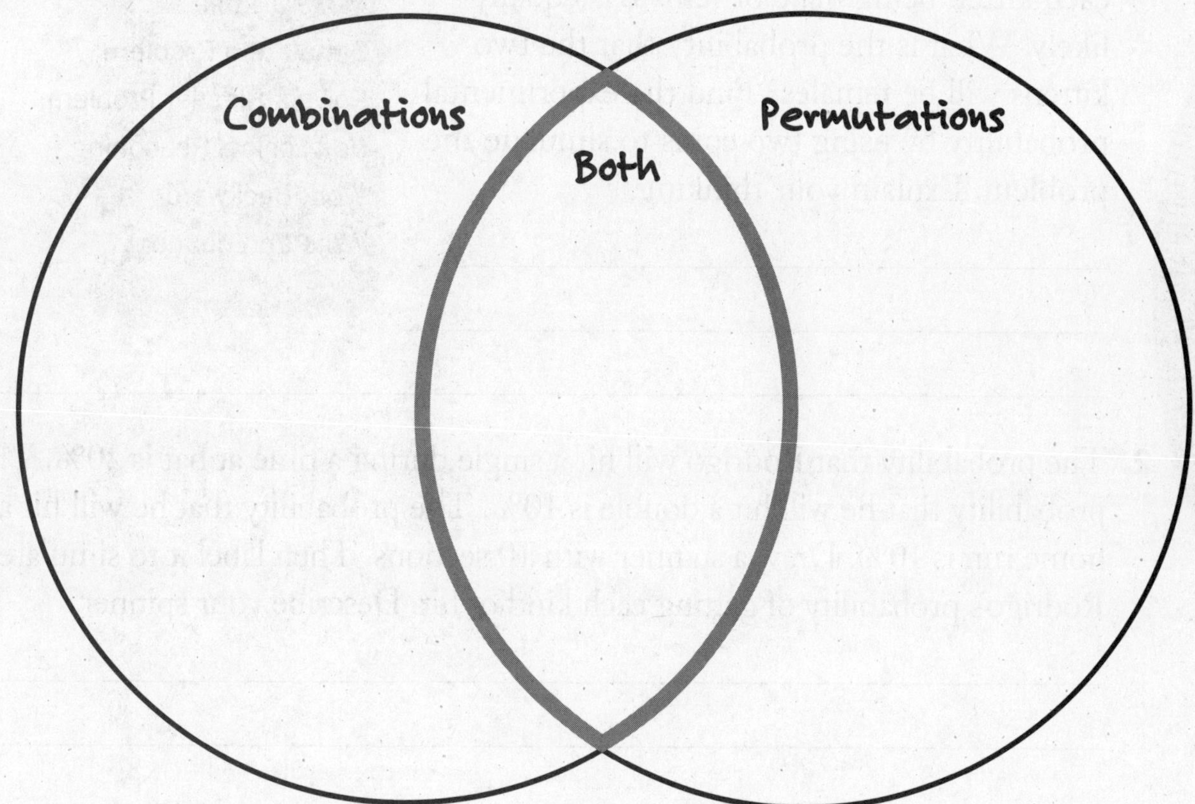

B. Clarifying Clarify the information in the Venn Diagram above. Write two or three sentences that tell how combinations and permutations differ.

Name

Problem Solving

Simulate a Problem

Use the strategy *simulate a problem* to solve these problems.

Problem-Solving Skills

- Draw a Diagram
- Guess, Check, and Revise
- Look for a Pattern
- Make an Organized List
- Make a Model
- Make a Table
- **Simulate a Problem**
- Solve a Simpler Problem
- Use Logical Reasoning
- Work Backward
- Write an Equation

1. A cat is expecting two kittens. The chance of each kitten being male or female is equally likely. What is the probability that the two kittens will be females? Find the experimental probability by using two coins to simulate the problem. Explain your thinking.

2. The probability that Rodrigo will hit a single during a time at bat is 20%. The probability that he will hit a double is 10%. The probability that he will hit a home run is 10%. Draw a spinner with 10 sections. Then label it to simulate Rodrigo's probability of getting each kind of hit. Describe your spinner.

My Summary of the Unit

Name ______________________________

Unit Vocabulary

Sentence Frames For each sentence below, choose one vocabulary term from the Word Bank. Write the same term in both blanks so that the sentence makes sense. Not all the terms will be used.

1. **aeimnoprttu** is one ________________ of the letters in the word ________________.

2. The ________________ of choosing **r** from the letters in the word ________________ is $\frac{1}{11}$.

3. It is ________________ to choose **t** from the letters in the word ________________.

4. **bcntm** is one 5-letter ________________ of the consonants in the word ________________.

5. If you choose two letters from the word ________________, one possible ________________ is **uc.**

6. You are ________________ to select **e** or **y** from the letters in the phrase ________________.

Word Bank

outcome	event
combination	probability
equally likely	permutation
tree diagram	impossible

Name ____________________

What Are Integers?

Practice

For Exercises 1–8, use the number line below.

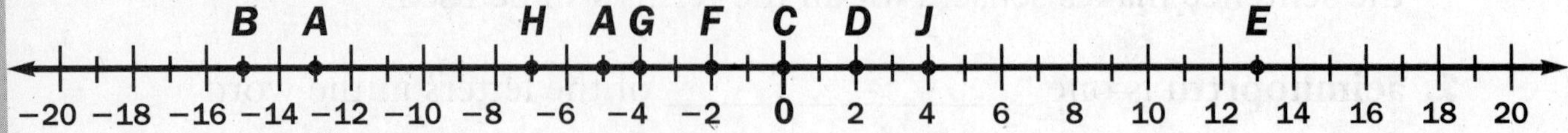

Name the point for each integer.

1. −7 ________ **2.** 13 ________ **3.** −15 ________ **4.** 2 ________

For Exercises 5–8, give the integer for each point. Then give the opposite and the absolute value for the integer.

	Point	Integer	Opposite	Absolute Value
5.	*C*			
6.	*F*			
7.	*G*			
8.	*J*			

For Exercises 9–11, use < or > to compare the integers.

9. 0 ________ −42 **10.** −3 ________ −17 **11.** −36 ________ 12

For Exercises 12 and 13, write the integers in order from least to greatest.

12. −5, −10, 15, −30, 20 ____________________

13. −12, 0, −3, −18, −29 ____________________

14. **Extended Response** Tell if the sentence below is always true, sometimes true, or never true. Explain and give examples to support your answer.

The absolute value of a positive integer is less than the absolute value of a negative integer. ____________________

____

____

Name ____________________

FOR USE WITH PAGE 260

Develop Language

A. Definition Chart Complete the Definition Chart below. Define each term and try to give three examples.

Term	Definition	Examples
counting numbers		
whole numbers		
integers		
positive integers		
negative integers		
zero		
opposites		
absolute value		

B. Identifying Identify the best term in the Word Bank to describe each situation. Write its letter in the blank. One word will be used twice.

Word Bank

a. positive integer
b. negative integer
c. zero
d. opposites
e. absolute value

____ The distance a car traveled

____ A golf score neither above nor below par

____ A football team's gain of 8 yards

____ A shipwreck 350 feet below sea level

____ A gain of \$5 and a loss of \$5

____ A mountain peak 7,000 meters above sea level

Name

Adding and Subtracting Integers

Practice

For Exercises 1–4, complete each sentence to tell what is shown by the chips. Remember, ⊕ represents 1 and ⊖ represents –1.

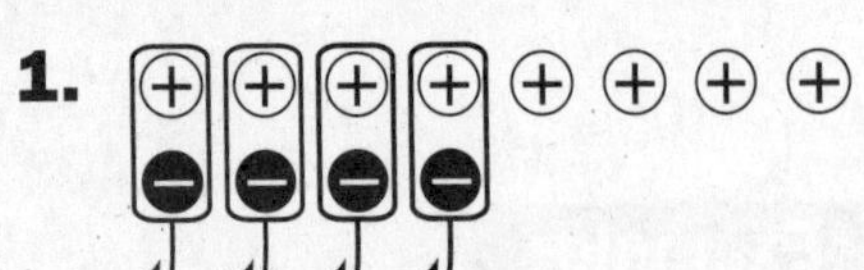

1. ____ + ____ = ______

2. ____ + ____ = ______

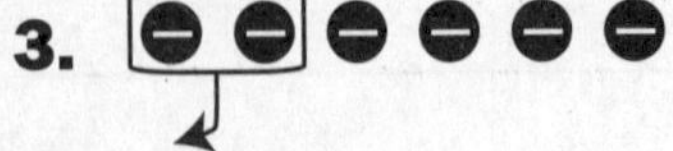

3. ____ – ____ = ______

4. ____ – ____ = ______

For Exercises 5–12, find each sum or difference.

5. $-12 + 4 =$ ______ **6.** $-16 - 16 =$ ______ **7.** $15 + (-6) =$ ______

8. $-36 + 36 =$ ______ **9.** $-10 - 5 =$ ______ **10.** $-11 - (-3) =$ ______

11. $14 - (-14) =$ ______ **12.** $-9 + (-13) =$ ______

Extended Response Tell whether each sentence is always true, sometimes true, or never true. If sometimes true, give two examples to support your answer.

13. The sum of two negative integers is negative. ____________________

____

14. The sum of a negative integer and a positive integer is positive.

____

____

15. The difference of two negative integers is negative.

____

____

Name ______________________

FOR USE WITH PAGE 265

Develop Language

A. Sentence Frames Use a term from the Word Bank to complete each sentence.

Word Bank	
absolute	negative
add	positive
difference	subtract
opposite	sum
zero	

1. The sum of 8 and 13 is a ______________ integer.

2. To ______________ 5 and −12, first find their ______________ values.

3. To ______________ −10 from another integer, add its ______________.

4. The integers 18 and −18 form a ______________ pair.

5. The ______________ of 0 − 4 is a ______________ integer.

B. Summarizing Use the terms in the Word Bank above to summarize these rules for adding and subtracting integers.

1. To add two integers with the same sign, add their ______________ values. The ______________ takes the sign of the two integers.

2. To add two integers with different signs, find the ______________ of their ______________ values. The ______________ takes the sign of the integer with the greater ______________ value.

3. To subtract an integer, ______________ its ______________.

Multiplying and Dividing Integers

Practice

For Exercises 1–4, complete each sentence to tell what is shown by the chips.

1. 

____ × ____ = ________

2. 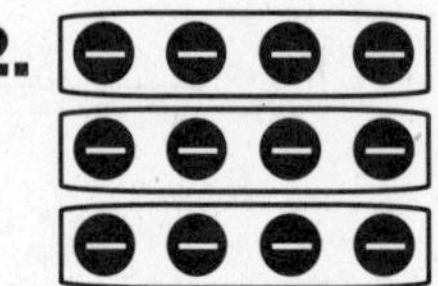

____ × ____ = ________

3. 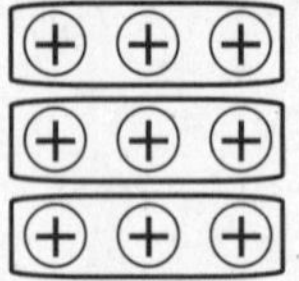

____ ÷ ____ = ________

4.

____ ÷ ____ = ________

For Exercises 5–12, find each product or quotient.

5. $-10 \times 2 =$ ________

6. $-8 \times (-6) =$ ________

7. $5 \times (-7) =$ ________

8. $32 \times 0 =$ ________

9. $-10 \div 5 =$ ________

10. $-28 \div (-4) =$ ________

11. $17 \div (-17) =$ ________

12. $0 \div 13 =$ ________

13. Simplify: $(-3)^4 \times (-10 + 2)$ ________

14. **Multiple Choice** Circle the letter of the correct choice.
The product of two negative integers is

A. less than either integer.

B. greater than either integer.

C. zero.

D. cannot tell

Name ______________________

FOR USE WITH PAGE 270

Develop Language

A. Fill In Use the fact that multiplication and division are inverse operations to complete each set of related equations.

1. $8 \times 3 =$ ________ $3 \times$ ________ $= 24$

$24 \div 8 =$ ________ $24 \div$ ________ $= 8$

2. $-4 \times 2 =$ ________ $2 \times$ ________ $= -8$

$-8 \div 2 =$ ________ $-8 \div$ ________ $= 2$

3. $-5 \times -4 =$ ________ $-4 \times$ ________ $= 20$

$20 \div -4 =$ ________ $20 \div$ ________ $= -4$

Complete each sentence with the words *positive* or *negative.*

4. If two integers have the same sign, their product and their quotient are ________________.

5. If two integers have opposite signs, their product and their quotient are ________________.

B. Organizing Complete these tables to organize what you know about adding and multiplying integers.

Adding Integers	Positive or Negative Sum?
both positive	positive
both negative	
one positive, one negative	

Multiplying Integers	Positive or Negative Product?
both positive	
both negative	
one positive, one negative	

The Coordinate Plane

Practice

For Exercises 1–11, use the coordinate plane on the right. Give the coordinates for each point or the point for each ordered pair.

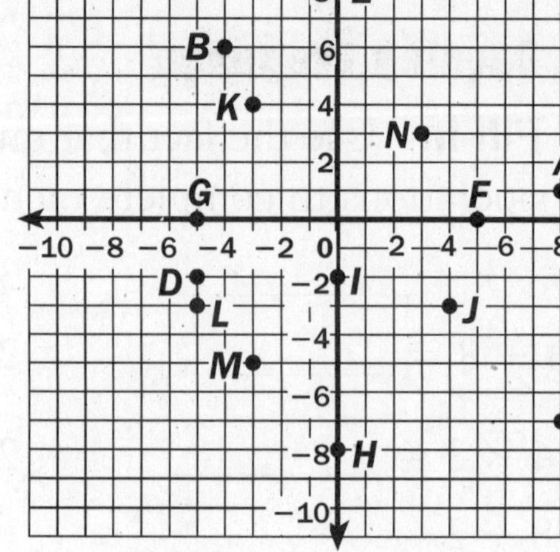

1. A __________

2. B __________

3. C __________ **4.** D __________ **5.** E __________

6. $(5, 0)$ __________ **7.** $(4, -3)$ __________ **8.** $(0, -2)$ __________

9. $(-3, -5)$ __________ **10.** $(-3, 4)$ __________ **11.** $(-5, 0)$ __________

For Exercises 12 and 13, choose four values for x and find the y value for each. Then graph the ordered pairs on the coordinate plane and draw a line through the points. Label each graph with its equation.

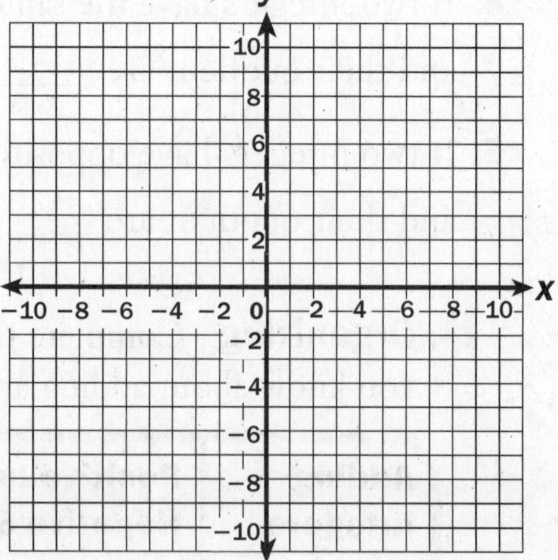

12. $y = -2x$

13. $y = 3x - 2$

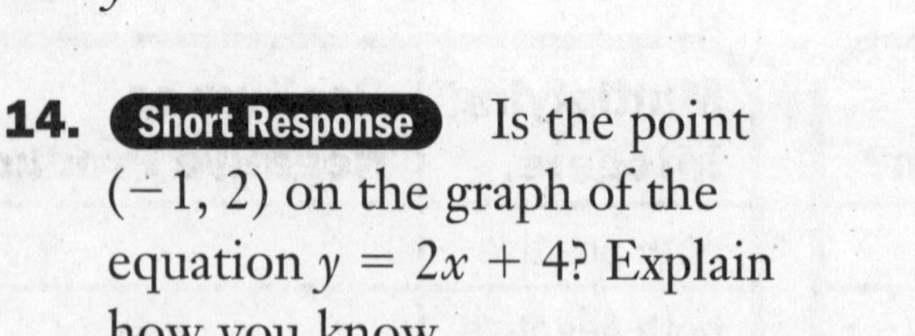

14. Short Response Is the point $(-1, 2)$ on the graph of the equation $y = 2x + 4$? Explain how you know.

____

____

____

____

Name ______________________________

FOR USE WITH PAGE 275

Develop Language

A. Labeling Label the parts of the coordinate plane with the correct term from the Word Bank.

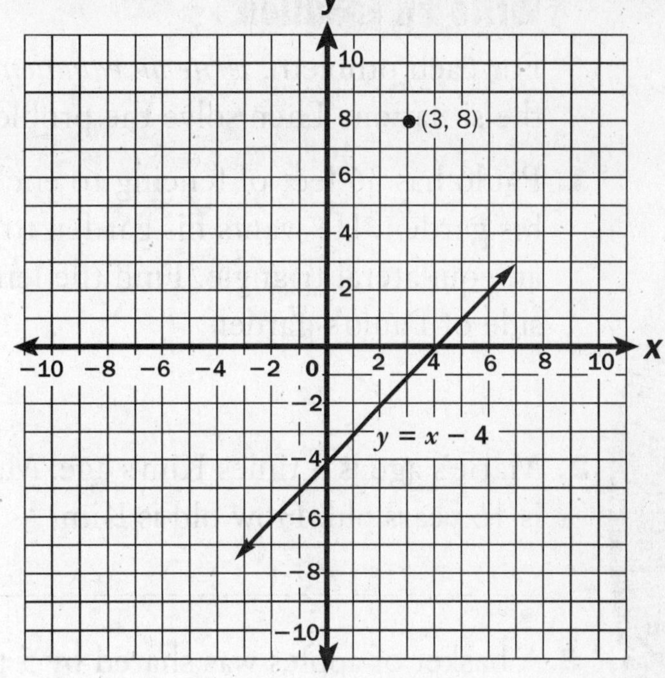

Word Bank

x-axis	y-axis
origin	ordered pair
Quadrant I	Quadrant II
Quadrant III	Quadrant IV
x-coordinate	y-coordinate
linear equation	

B. Explaining The graphs on the coordinate plane on the right are labeled with their equations. Explain how the graphs are alike and different. Then explain how the equations are alike and different.

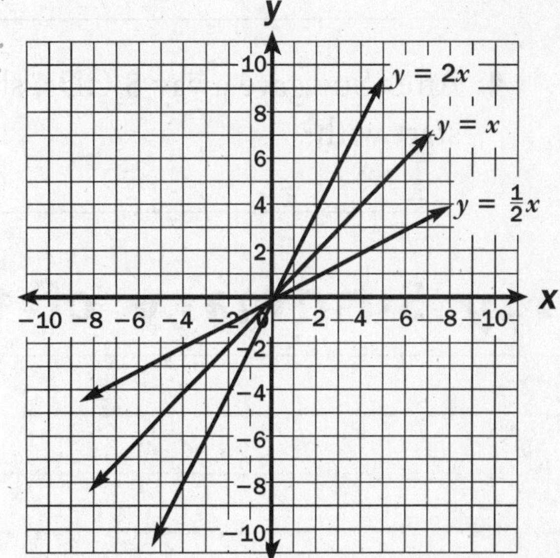

____

____

____

____

____

____

____

Name

Problem Solving

Write an Equation

For each problem, *write an equation* to describe the situation. Then solve the problem.

Problem-Solving Skills

- Draw a Diagram
- Guess, Check, and Revise
- Look for a Pattern
- Make an Organized List
- Make a Model
- Make a Table
- Simulate a Problem
- Solve a Simpler Problem
- Use Logical Reasoning
- Work Backward
- **Write an Equation**

1. Paulo has 36 feet of fencing to enclose his garden. He wants his garden to be an equilateral triangle. Find the length of each side of Paulo's garden.

2. Marie's age is 4 times Kim's age. Marie is 16 years old. How old is Kim?

3. A basket of apples was shared by 5 people. Each person received 7 apples. How many apples were in the basket?

4. After Sue gave away 8 CDs, she had 23 CDs left. How many CDs did Sue start with?

My Summary of the Unit

Name ______________________________

FOR USE WITH PAGES 256–277

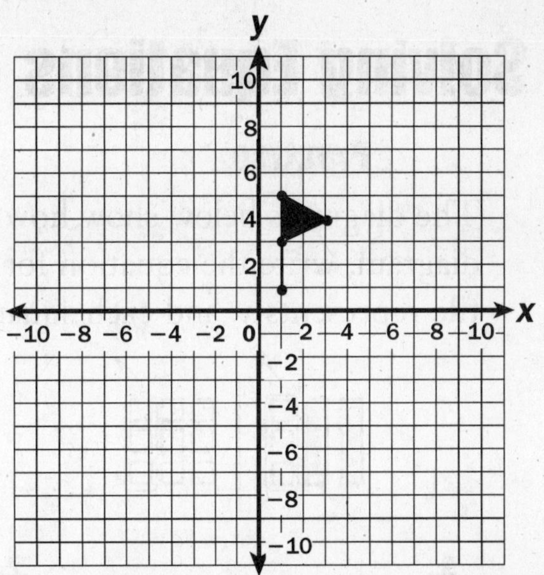

Unit Vocabulary

Flags in Motion The points (1, 1), (1, 5), (3, 4), and (1, 3) have been connected on the grid to form a flag. Complete the table below. Always start with the original coordinates. Use words from the Word Bank to describe the change in the flag. Draw the new flags.

Directions	New Coordinates	Change in Flag
Multiply each x-coordinate by −1 and each y-coordinate by 1.	(−1, 1) (−1, 5) (−3, 4) (−1, 3)	Flag is flipped, or reflected, over the y-axis into Quadrant II.
Multiply both coordinates by −1.		
Add −9 to each coordinate.		
Add 7 to the x-coordinate and 2 to the y-coordinate.		
Multiply each coordinate by 2.		

Word Bank

vertical	x-axis	quadrant	rotated
horizontal	y-axis	reflected	translated

Name

Solving Equations

Practice

The diagrams below show how to solve a two-operation equation. For each diagram, write the equation for the step of the solution shown. Each shaded tile represents x, and each square tile represents 1.

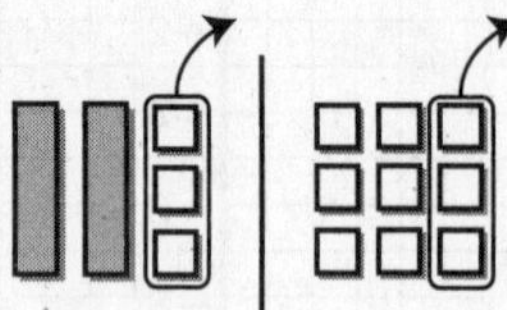

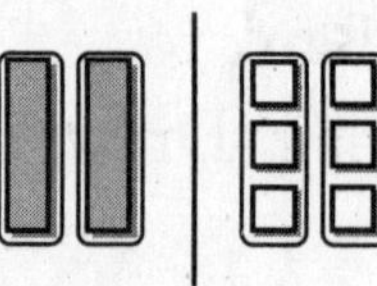

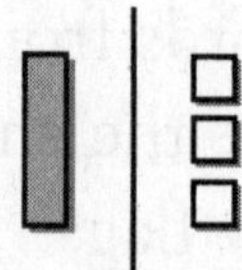

1. ______________ **2.** ______________ **3.** ______________

For Exercises 4–17, solve and check each equation.

4. $34 + y = 17$ ______________

5. $n - 25 = 25$ ______________

6. $\frac{s}{6} = \frac{7}{12}$ ______________

7. $13t = 13$ ______________

8. $32 = x + 19$ ______________

9. $120 = 8m$ ______________

10. $5a + 3 = 18$ ______________

11. $3s - 12 = 18$ ______________

12. $23 = 5y - 17$ ______________

13. $7n + 2 = 65$ ______________

14. $\frac{r}{6} - 4 = 3$ ______________

15. $23 = 11 + \frac{c}{4}$ ______________

16. $\frac{a}{3} + 6 = 18$ ______________

17. $\frac{x}{5} - 9 = 11$ ______________

Multiple Choice For Exercises 18–20, circle the correct solution.

18. $26 - 2a = 18$

A. $a = 22$ **B.** $a = 4$ **C.** $a = 8$

19. $30 - 3x = 3$

A. $x = 11$ **B.** $x = 10$ **C.** $x = 9$

20. $\frac{m}{9} - 2 = 16$

A. $m = 162$ **B.** $m = 81$ **C.** $m = 32$

Name ______________________________

FOR USE WITH PAGE 282

Develop Language

A. Steps Tell what step or steps you must take to solve each equation. Then give the solution.

Equation	Step or Steps	Solution
$x - 5 = 45$		
$\frac{n}{8} = 8$		
$8s - 12 = 36$		
$6 + \frac{n}{3} = 27$		
$\frac{x}{4} - 8 = 16$		
$10 + 6n = 34$		

B. Justifying Complete the solution for this equation, and give reasons for the steps. Choose your reasons from this list: *Addition Property of Equality, Subtraction Property of Equality, Multiplication Property of Equality, Division Property of Equality, simplify.*

$6m - 15 = 15$

$6m - 15 + 15 = 15$ ________ ____________________

$6m =$ ________ ____________________

$6m \div 6 = 30$ ________ ____________________

$m =$ ________ ____________________

Name

Inequalities

Practice

For Exercises 1 and 2, write the inequality.

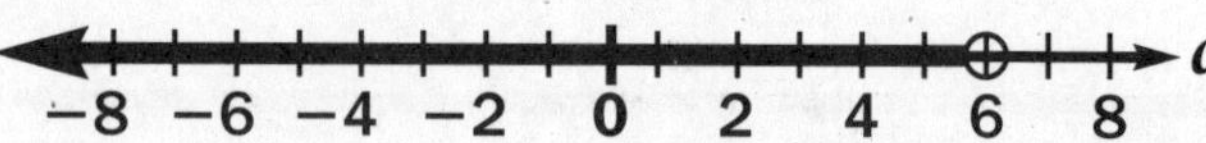

1. ______________________ **2.** ______________________

For Exercises 3–6, solve and graph each inequality.

3. $x - 4 \geq 2$

4. $5y < 25$

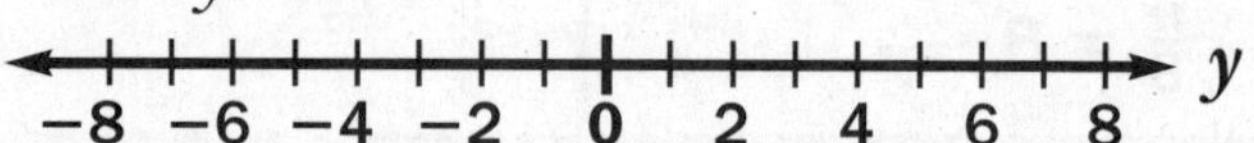

5. $8 > m + 3$

6. $\frac{n}{2} \leq -2$

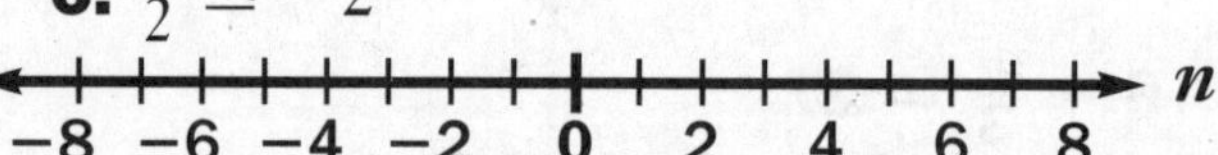

For Exercises 7–15, solve each inequality and give two solutions that check.

7. $2 + x > -4$ ______________

8. $\frac{c}{3} \leq 6$ ______________

9. $n - 8 \geq -5$ ______________

10. $3m < 24$ ______________

11. $-4 + f \leq -4$ ______________

12. $36 \leq 12x$ ______________

13. $g - 9 \geq 0$ ______________

14. $16 \leq \frac{x}{4}$ ______________

15. $12 < 8 + b$ ______________

16. **Short Response** Are −15 and −20 solutions to $y + 40 \leq 25$? Explain how you know. ____

Name ____________________

FOR USE WITH PAGE 287

Develop Language

A. Definition Chart Complete the Definition Chart below. Define each term and give a numerical example.

Symbol	Definition	Example
$\neq$		
$<$		
$\leq$		
$>$		
$\geq$		

B. Comparing Graph each inequality on the number line beside it.

$x > 2$ –5 –4 –3 –2 –1 0 1 2 3 4 5

$2 > x$ –5 –4 –3 –2 –1 0 1 2 3 4 5

$x \geq 2$ –5 –4 –3 –2 –1 0 1 2 3 4 5

$2 \geq x$ –5 –4 –3 –2 –1 0 1 2 3 4 5

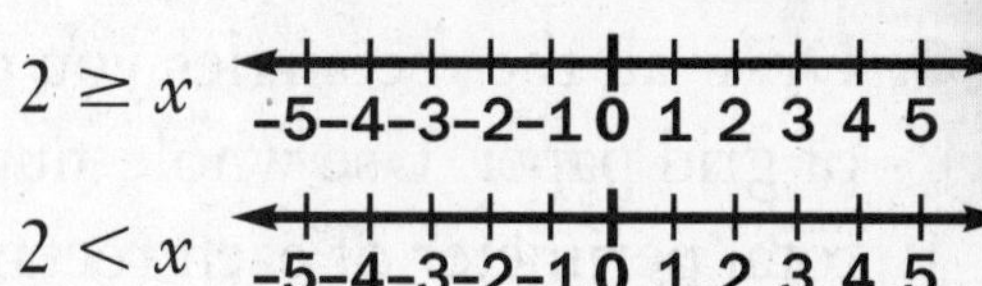

$x < 2$ –5 –4 –3 –2 –1 0 1 2 3 4 5

$2 < x$ –5 –4 –3 –2 –1 0 1 2 3 4 5

$x \leq 2$ –5 –4 –3 –2 –1 0 1 2 3 4 5

$2 \leq x$ –5 –4 –3 –2 –1 0 1 2 3 4 5

Compare each pair of the inequalities. Tell how they are alike and how they are different.

$x > 2$ and $x \geq 2$ ____________________

$x > 2$ and $x < 2$ ____________________

$x \leq 2$ and $2 \geq x$ ____________________

$x \geq 2$ and $2 \geq x$ ____________________

Name

Problem Solving

Make a Model

Sometimes you can *make a model* to help you understand how to solve a problem. Using actual objects can help you model a situation.

Problem-Solving Skills

- Draw a Diagram
- Guess, Check, and Revise
- Look for a Pattern
- Make an Organized List
- **Make a Model**
- Make a Table
- Simulate a Problem
- Solve a Simpler Problem
- Use Logical Reasoning
- Work Backward
- Write an Equation

1. Arrange 7 counters as shown. Then add a second and third ring of counters. How many counters are in each ring?

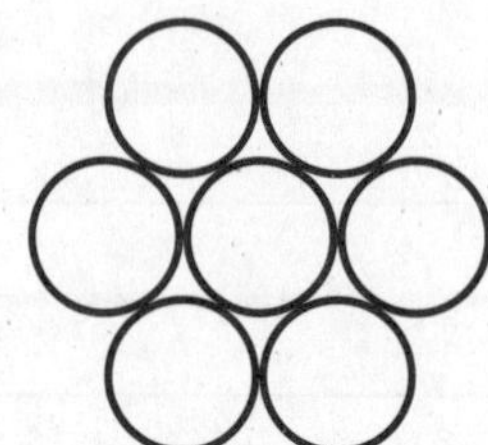

a. 1st ________________

b. 2nd ________________ **c.** 3rd ________________

d. Predict the number of counters in the 4th ring. ________________

2. There is a student in front of and behind Beth in the lunch line. Carl is second in line. The same number of people are in front of and behind Amy. Two people are between Beth and Dee. Use slips of paper labeled *Amy*, *Beth*, *Carl*, *Dee*, and *Ed* to model this situation and to tell the students' positions in the line. ________________

3. Draw all the rectangles you can with an area of 36 square units on a sheet of grid paper. Use whole-number side lengths. List the dimensions and total perimeter of each rectangle. Which rectangle has the least perimeter? The greatest? ________________

My Summary of the Unit

Name

FOR USE WITH PAGES 278–289

Unit Vocabulary

Number Lines The number line below shows the graphs of the solutions to the equations and inequalities given below. Label each graph with the variable it represents. Then describe each graph using vocabulary from the unit: *variable*, *solution*, *two-operation equation*, and *inequality*.

$5a - 4 = 26$	$b \geq 12$	$\frac{c}{2} = 5$
$d < -13$	$7e + 21 = 21$	$\frac{f}{2} + 2 = -2$

a:

b:

c:

d:

e:

f:

Solve each inequality and then graph it on a number line.

$8m \geq 40$ ____________

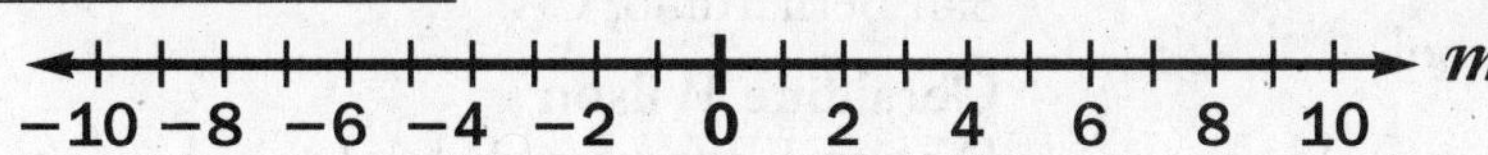

$n - 6 < -12$ ____________

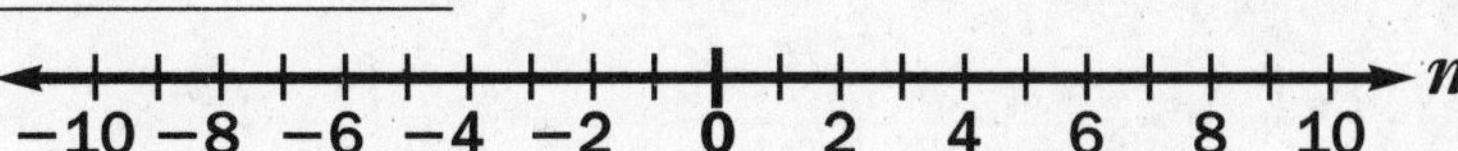

$\frac{s}{2} > -4$ ____________

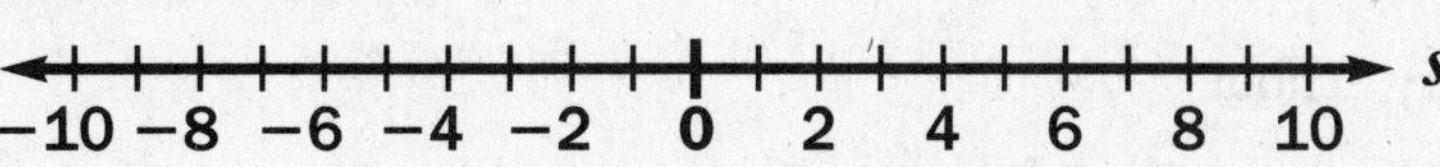

CONSULTANTS

Shane Bassett
Mill Park Elementary School
David Douglas School District
Portland, OR

Jeanette Gordon
Senior Educational Consultant
Illinois Resource Center
Des Plaines, IL

Dr. Aixa Perez-Prado
College of Education
Florida International University
Miami, FL

Dennis Terdy
Director of Grants and Special Programs, Newcomer Center
Township High School
Arlington Heights, IL

TEACHER GROUP REVIEWERS

Sara Ainsworth
Hannah Beardsley Middle School
Crystal Lake, IL

Walter A. Blair
Otis Elementary School
Chicago, IL

Vincent U. Egonmwan
Joyce Kilmer Elementary School
Chicago, IL

Anne Hopkins
Arie Crown School
Skokie, IL

Heather Pusich
Field Middle School
Northbrook, IL

Dana Robinson
Prairie Crossing Charter School
Grayslake, IL

Nestor Torres
Chase Elementary School
Chicago, IL

RESEARCH SITE LEADERS

Carmen Concepción
Lawton Chiles Middle School
Miami, FL

Andrea Dabbs
Edendale Middle School
San Lorenzo, CA

Daniel Garcia
Public School 130
Bronx, NY

Bobbi Ciriza Houtchens
Arroyo Valley High School
San Bernardino, CA

Portia McFarland
Wendell Phillips High School
Chicago, IL

RESEARCH SITE MATH REVIEWERS

Maritza Baez
Lawton Chiles Middle School
Miami, FL

Andrew Dunbar, Jr.
M.S. 201 STAR Academy
Bronx, NY

Elizabeth Heckman
Edendale Middle School
San Lorenzo, CA

Teri Paine
Martin Luther King, Jr. Middle School
San Bernardino, CA

Geraldine Wilson
Warren Elementary School
Chicago, IL

MATH TEACHER REVIEWERS

Anita Bright
Fairfax County Public Schools
Fairfax, VA

Bridgette Calloway-Hall
O'Farrell Community School
San Diego, CA

Renée Crawford
O'Farrell Community School
San Diego, CA

Roberta Girardi
Howard County Public Schools
Ellicott City, MD

Velia Gomez
Gilmore Middle School
Racine, WI

Abdullahi Mohamed
Sanford Middle School
Minneapolis, MN

Steve Paterwic
High School of Science and Technology
Springfield, MA

Mario Perez
Newcomer Center/School District 214
Arlington Heights, IL

Cristina Sanchez-Lopez
Illinois Resource Center
Des Plaines, IL

ACKNOWLEDGMENTS

Photo Credits

3 left © Eileen Ryan Photography, 2004 *3 right* © Eileen Ryan Photography, 2004 *3 bottom* ©Royalty-Free/CORBIS *3 bottom* © Eileen Ryan Photography, 2004
Front Cover Foreground: Photodisc/Getty Images; **Background:** Photodisc/Getty Images; BrandX/Getty Images; Based on a system of labeling the columns A through J and the rows 1 through 18, the following background images were taken by the following photographers: A2, A5, A6, A15, A17, A18, B13, B14, B16, C1, C6, C7, C16, D2 D5, D13, D15, E1, E3, E4, E6, E8, E9, E16, E17, E18, F1, F4, F8, F9, F13, F15, F18, H1, H2, H4, H9, H13, H17, I1, I3, I5, I7, I8, I10, I12, I14, I15, J3, J4, J8, J9, J13, J15: Philip Coblentz/Getty Images; B3: Spike Mafford/Getty Images; E5: Albert J Copley/Getty Images; F5, J7: Steve Allen/Getty Images; F12: Sexto Sol/Getty Images 47, 105, 152, 212, 227